ISBN 978-1-332-11754-3
PIBN 10286977

1 MONTH OF
FREE
READING

at

www.ForgottenBooks.com

By purchasing this book you are eligible for one month membership to ForgottenBooks.com, giving you unlimited access to our entire collection of over 700,000 titles via our web site and mobile apps.

To claim your free month visit:

www.forgottenbooks.com/free286977

English
Français
Deutsche
Italiano
Español
Português

www.forgottenbooks.com

Mythology Photography **Fiction**
Fishing Christianity **Art** Cooking
Essays Buddhism Freemasonry
Medicine **Biology** Music **Ancient**
Egypt Evolution Carpentry Physics
Dance Geology **Mathematics** Fitness
Shakespeare **Folklore** Yoga Marketing
Confidence Immortality Biographies
Poetry **Psychology** Witchcraft
Electronics Chemistry History **Law**
Accounting **Philosophy** Anthropology
Alchemy Drama Quantum Mechanics
Atheism Sexual Health **Ancient History**
Entrepreneurship Languages Sport
Paleontology Needlework Islam
Metaphysics Investment Archaeology
Parenting Statistics Criminology
Motivational

THE
COURTRIGHT (KORTRIGHT) FAMILY

DESCENDANTS OF

BASTIAN VAN KORTRYK,

A Native of Belgium who Emigrated to Holland about 1615

BY JOHN HOWARD ABBOTT

ILLUSTRATED

TOBIAS A. WRIGHT
Printer and Publisher
150 Bleecker Street, New York
1922

☆ ❋ cs

'9 ²

History

ILLUSTRATIONS

INTRODUCTION

This book, the result of twenty years research during leisure time, may be of some assistance to those of other branches of the Courtright family who are not familiar with its history, but it is by no means complete, nor free from errors.

It is more especially designed to preserve a genealogy of Benjamin Cortright, through his sons Cornelius, Henry and John, who came from Minisink district in Northampton County soon after the Revolution and settled in Plains, Luzerne County, Pennsylvania, in the Wyoming Valley, leaving descendants now widely dispersed. It also includes a partial genealogy of the descendants of Elisha Cortright, a cousin, who came to the Valley at an early date.

Records of the Harlem branch of the family herein contained have been taken literally from the accurate and well written "History of Harlem" by James Riker, and from numerous other authorities, while all baptisms and early marriages will be found in the published records of the Reformed Dutch churches of New Amsterdam, Kingston, Rochester, Sleepy Hollow, Wawarsing, Smithfield, Machackemeck, (Deerpark) Walpeck and other places.

The sketches of the Abbott and Gore families are largely quotations from Oscar J. Harvey's History of Wilkes-Barre, Pa., while much information has been gleaned from the publications of the New York Genealogical and Biographical Society, the Pennsylvania Archives, and many other sources.

There are Cortrights among the early generations of whom nothing more will ever be known than name and date of baptism, some of whom died young, and others who married and may be traced through generations now unrecorded.

Many children were born, of whom there is no record, owing to frequent migration of young couples to new settlements where there was no established church, and in many instances church records have been lost or destroyed, containing information of great value.

Duplication of given names was frequent among our Dutch ancestors, making it difficult to ascertain with certainty who was referred to in marriage records, but these have been determined by comparisons of ages, locations, names of children, etc., so far as possible, although it will be surprising if no errors are discovered. Information of Cortright families unrecorded here, correction of errors and supplied omissions will be gratefully received and recorded in a future edition. The arrangement of this book is so simple as to require no explanation, while the abbreviations are those generally used, such as b., for born, bap., baptized, m., married; d., died; j. m., single man; j. d., single woman, etc.

Our Cortright ancestors were mostly farmers, living simple lives, industrious and honest, of strong religious convictions, sharing with other pioneers the dangers and hardships incident to the settlement of a new country, and but very few attained distinction.

My warmest feelings of gratitude and sincere thanks are tendered to those who have so kindly aided me by supplying the necessary data, thus making this work possible, and not in a single instance has it been refused or my inquiries ignored.

Your compiler is amply compensated in the thought that this record may afford pleasure to the Courtright descendants by giving them reliable information of their ancestors, heretofore not available to many, and foster an honest pride in an honorable American ancestry of two hundred and sixty years.

Your Kinsman,

JOHN HOWARD ABBOTT,

4140 Agnes Avenue,

Kansas City, Mo.

April 16th, 1922.

THE FAMILY NAME

Family names were the exception and not the rule among our early Dutch colonists. The mass of people in the Fatherland used only a patronymic, formed by adding to the child's Christian name that of the father, with the affix, sen or son, by which originated all names so terminating, as for example, Hendrick Jansen (Hendrick, son of Jan), and the like.

In correct writing, the affix was often shortened to se, or z, and always in the case of females, to s. This custom necessarily produced among the male descendants of the same progenitor a diversity of surnames, if they may, for convenience, be so called.

Thus, Cornelius and Hendrick, being sons of Jan Bastiaensen, would be known as Cornelius Jansen and Hendrick Jansen, while their children would be named respectively Cornelissen and Hendricksen, and these names in turn each afford other varieties in the next generation.

On the other hand, the use of the patronymic caused a frequent recurrence of the same name where no family connection whatever existed.

The inconvenience thus arising, and particularly the liability of confounding persons of a similar name, was partially obviated by the practice in vogue in Fatherland, kept up by the colonists, both in familiar speech and in formal writings, of distinguishing persons by their birthplace, as for example, Hendrick Jansen Van Kortryk, that is, Hendrick Jansen, from or of Kortryk.

In the Kingston and other church records, our ancestors were called Jansen and Hendricksen, until 1703, when the name was recorded Kortright, with many ways of spelling it.

This valued link connecting the colonist with his former home, was in many cases directly to his interest to preserve.

In Holland, as with us, the name of the place thus often became the permanent family name, of which many instances abound, but it often resulted that two brothers, born in different places, and from these deriving their respective surnames, gave rise to as many families, whose common origin, after a few generations, none would suspect.

In many cases the "Van" has been dropped, and often the name so changed as to disguise its origin, as those of Oblinus and Kortright.

The first of these, derived from Houplines, and after emigration, probably in conformity to English utterance, became Oblinus, and by usage before mentioned, written Van Oblinus, and at first, the Kortrights also used the Van. The Kortright name appears in the ancient land and church records in various forms, as Van Kortryk, Kortregt, Kortrecht, Kortreght, etc., and frequently beginning with the letter C, and spelled phonetically by the ministers to whom children were brought for baptism, or young couples presenting themselves for marriage. There were other variants, such as Curtright, and rarely Cartright, but soon after the Revolution, the name was written Cortright by most of the descendants, although now generally written Courtright.

Very few names among us at present, whether of Dutch, French or other descent, preserve their original form, a result to be deprecated, though a return to the early orthography may now neither be practicable nor desirable.

THE COURTRIGHT FAMILY

Kortryk (in French, Courtrai) was the home of the earliest ancestor of the Courtright (Kortright) family of which there is any knowledge, so a brief history of the town may be of interest to those who desire information regarding the genealogy of this family.

Kortryk is situated twenty-six miles Southwest of Ghent, on the river Lys, in the Province of West Flanders, Belgium, and is celebrated for its fine linen, while its lace factories are also important, employing many of its inhabitants. In 1910 it had a population of about 36,000, but considerable as is the prosperity of modern Courtrai, it is but a shadow of what it was in the middle ages during the halcyon period of the Flemish communes, as then it had a population of over 200,000.

Many interesting structures of Courtrai's former grandeur remain; the Pont de Broel, with its towers at either end of the bridge, is as characteristic and complete as any monument of ancient Flanders that has come down to modern times.

Among the remarkable public buildings is the Hotel de Ville, or Town Hall, a Gothic edifice, built in 1526, containing two singularly carved chimney pieces, representing the Virtues and Vices, and events in the early history of the town, one of them decorated with the coats of arms of the allied towns of Ghent and Bruges, the standard bearers of the Knights of Kortryk, and various statues, including those of Arch Duke Albert and his wife. The church of St. Martin dates from the fifteenth century, but the most important building in Courtrai is the church of Notre Dame, begun by Count Baldwin IX in 1191, and completed in 1211, in the chapel of which is hung one of Van Dyck's masterpieces, "The Erection of the Cross," and in this church are several other celebrated paintings.

The Flemish language differs but slightly from the Dutch, in the middle ages forming but one tongue, and even at the present time the Flemish spoken language differs no more from the Dutch than some German dialects do from each other.

The country called Belgium at the present time, originally peopled by a race of Celtic origin and subsequently overrun by Teutonic invaders, was conquered by Caesar, at which time the town existed and under the Romans was called Cortoriacum, afterwards changed to Curtricum. The Salic Franks gained possession in the fifth century, and in the ninth, the country formed part of the empire of Charlemagne.

Kortryk was destroyed by the Normans, but rebuilt by Baldwin III, of Flanders, in the tenth century, who endowed it with market rights and laid the foundation of its industrial importance by inviting the settlement of foreign weavers.

Flanders carried on a long continuous struggle against France, the result of which was the establishment of its complete independence.

On the 11th of July, 1302, below the walls of Kortryk, was fought the famous battle of the Spurs, when the French army of 47,000 men, under the Count of Artois, was defeated by the army of the allied burghers of Bruges, Ypres and Kortryk, consisting of 20,000 men, under Count John of Nabur and Duke William of Juliers.

The French army was put to flight, while upward of 1,200 knights and several thousand soldiers fell, and afterward the victors collected over seven hundred golden spurs, an appendage worn by the French knights alone, which they hung up as a trophy in the church of the convent of Groenangen, now destroyed. A small chapel outside the Ghent gate, erected in 1831, marks the center of the battlefield.

On the extinction of the male line of the Counts of Flanders in 1385, it became annexed to Burgundy by the marriage of Philip the Bold with a daughter of the Flemish princely race. The splendor loving Philip the Bold employed artists of every kind, while the name of his grand-son, Philip the Good, 1419-1467, is inseparably connected with the first bloom of Flemish painting.

In 1477 the Netherlands came into the possession of the House of Hapsburg, Charles V., grand-son of Maximilian, succeeding to the whole of these provinces, which on his abdication in 1555, came under the sway of his son, Philip II, and thenceforward the Netherlands were subject to Spanish supremacy.

About this time the new doctrines of the Reformed religion began to spread among the people, many of them embracing its teachings, more especially the thinking and sober classes, who had discarded their old beliefs and superstitions, and who were known as Walloons.

The religious reform was rife not only in the Netherlands, but in England, France and Germany as well, and met with deadly opposition from the ruling powers, civil and ecclesiastical, being subjected to every cruel means for its suppression that these could exert, among which was the infamous system of espionage and torture known as the Spanish Inquisition.

In 1559 the burdensome presence of the Spanish troops and other grievances led to numerous tumults, to suppress which the King dispatched the Duke of Alva to the Netherlands with an army of 20,000 men.

The persecutions under the royal governor, the bloody Duke of Alva, had become so insufferable, that in 1568 the provinces broke out in revolt, and took up arms under the noble patriot, William of Orange, but at first without success.

Brighter were the prospects when, eight years later, the Walloons again struck for their liberties, for unable longer to bear the outrages heaped upon them, they appealed to arms, joining the Hollanders and French Huguenots in the effort to drive the Spaniards from the country and enjoy religious toleration.

As a sequence, Holland, Zeeland, Gelderland and other provinces achieved their independence in 1579, after a long and obstinate struggle, but the remaining Netherlands, part unwilling, part unable to shake off their fetters, relapsed into a more servile bondage to Spain and the Papacy, and the Protestant Walloons were allowed two years in which either to return to the bosom of the church or leave the country, so shut up in this alternative, thousands sought safety in flight.

The breaking out of war between France and Spain in 1635 also caused a considerable influx of Protestant refugees to England and Holland, and resulted in the conquest of parts of Flanders and other provinces and their annexation to France.

No class of Gallic blood was more remarkable than the Walloons, mainly included within France and Belgium. Theirs was a belt of country extending eastward from the river Lys, beyond both the Scheldt and Meuse, and embracing French or Walloon Flanders, most of Artois, the Cambresis, Hainault, Namur, Southern Brabant, and parts of Liege and Sedan, a fruitful region, and in the sixteenth century an independent Protestant state, attracting many of the persecuted Walloons during the religious troubles of that period.

The northern limits of the Walloon country would have been nearly defined by a line drawn from Liege, on the Meuse, to Calais; on the south it was bounded by Picardy, Champagne and Lorraine, provinces which at that time composed the French frontier.

The Walloon emigrations of the sixteenth century went largely by way of the Scheldt, the Meuse, and their affluents, to Holland.

Skirting interiorwise the districts which were the homes of the refugees, the Meuse flowed northerly, then swept westward around Brabant, reaching the sea by several outlets between the insular parts of South Holland. It is unsurpassed for bold and grand scenery, which beginning near Sedan, is heightened to the sublime as it reaches Namur where the Sambre enters it.

Towering walls of rock, now bare, now clad in foliage, rise on either side, while here and there huge cleft or ravine opens to view some far-reaching and romantic vale or dark unfathomed dell—fitting retreat for those stern feudal chiefs, who once took tribute of each passing vessel.

Weird stories are woven around its fantastic forms and crumbling castles of an early period, but stranger tales were those of the sixteenth century—of crafts richly freighted, but not with merchandise, stealing down its favoring current, bearing the victims of persecution, Protestant Walloons from the adjacent districts, to a land of safety.

The Walloons were a hardy, long lived race, tall, stout and muscular, of strong intellects, manly bearings, a sagacious, practical and laborious people, noted for the plainness of their tastes, manners and dress. These several traits were clearly traceable to their ancestors, the old Belgae, their descent from whom was also unmistakable in their coolness and pertinacity, in contrast to those of Celtic blood.

It was these qualities, combined with a natural love of arms, and the courage inherited from their ancestors, whom Caesar describes as the bravest of the Gauls, that made the Walloons such famous soldiers. Ever tenacious of their rights, and thus excessively litigant, they were yet hospitable and social, possessing much of the French vivacity. In domestic life they lacked no element of solid, home-spun comfort; the plain substantial domicile, roofed with tile or thatch, a bare floor, but a genial hearth-stone, with ample pile of blazing wood; the oaken board, set with brown ware or pewter, with goodly supply of simple, wholesome food—this satisfied the Walloon in the line of living, while song or instrumental music, of which they were very fond, enlivened the social hour.

Says Davies, the historian of Holland, "Nor was it more in the numbers than in the sort of population that Holland found her advantage. The fugitives were not criminals escaped from justice, speculators lured by the hope of plunder, nor idlers coming thither to enjoy the luxuries which their own country did not afford; they were generally men persecuted on account of their love of civic liberty, or their devotion to their religious tenets. Had they been content to sacrifice the one or the other to their present ease and interest they had remained unmolested where they were. It was by their activity, integrity and resolution that they rendered themselves obnoxious to the tyrannical and bigoted governments which drove them from their native land, and these virtues they carried with them to their adopted country, peopling it, not with vagabonds or indolent voluptuaries, but with brave intelligent and useful citizens."

Amsterdam, as the great commercial mart of Holland, and the seat of the Dutch West India Company, had become the great point of embark ation for colonists going to New Netherland. They came from all parts of the country, not only the native Dutch, but fugitives from France and the Netherlands, and also refugees from the German and Scandin- avian countries, seeking a home in the United Provinces.

Kortryk was a Flemish town yet farther down the Lys, which within the previous century had witnessed cruel persecutions, and during the existing war (how great its calamities) had changed hands four times in five years. But one of its families had escaped these last troubles by leaving some years before; we refer to the ancestors of the Kort- right (or Courtright) family, in its day, one of the most wealthy in landed possessions in Harlem, now part of New York City.

The large emigration to New Netherland from the exposed borders nearest the Spanish possessions, and especially the insular district having on the south the river Waal, and on the north the Rhine and Leck, furnished Harlem with several substantial families.

Central of the district mentioned, upon the small river Linge, which empties into the Waal, stood the city of Leerdam, giving name to a country in which it was situated—a level, grazing country, otherwise called the Prince's land, because inherited by a son of William of Orange. To Leerdam had retired the family of Sebastian, or Bastian Van Kort- ryk, about all we know of this Kortright progenitor with his royal Spanish name. Two sons of Bastian, of whom we must speak, Jan and Michiel, were born at Leerdam; but the first married and settled some further up the Linge, at a busy little village within sight of Wolfswaert Castle, as also of the ruined abbey of Marienwaert and called Beest, its bailiwick of the same name joining westerly to the Prince's land, but within the Gelderland border.

Michiel, or as often called, 'Chiel Kortright, the other son of Bastian, had also married and been living in the Prince's land, near Schoonre- woerd, a pretty village two miles northerly from Leerdam.

The spirit of emigration reaching this locality, many of its people began to pack up and leave for New Netherland, in which they had a safe precedent in no less a personage than the village pedagogue—much rever- enced was he and looked up to in those days,—good Master Gideon Schaets, who had gone thither in 1652, to preach the Gospel and fill the office of schoolmaster for young and old.

Every bit of news wafted home from time to time in friendly letters served to quicken interest in the new country which had caused so many vacant tenements and broken families about Beest and Schoonrewoerd.

Yet 'Chiel Bastiaensen tarried some years at Schoonrewoerd, till blessed with three or four children, when he, and his elder brother, Jan Bastiaensen, whose three sons, born at Beest, his humble home in a bend of the Linge, were fast approaching manhood, yielded to the flattering offers held out by the colonists, and agreed to leave for that distant land.

Proceeding to Amsterdam, they all embarked April 16th, 1663, in the ship Bonte-koe (Brindle or Spotted Cow), Jan Bergen, Master, in which ship there also sailed several French refugees from Mannheim, in the Palatinate. Men, women and children, there were ninety odd passengers, the French composing a third. Each adult was charged 39 florins, children under ten, half price, and it cost Jan Bastiaensen (Kort right) for himself, wife and family, 204 florins, 10 stivers.

The Bastiaensen brothers, upon their arrival, first went to Stuyvesant's Bowery, though they soon after came to Harlem.

Jan Bastiaensen, (born 1618) as we have seen, came to this country from the County of Leerdam, or the Prince's land, in South Holland, in 1663, accompanied by his brother, Michiel Bastiaensen, (born 1620), both of whom afterwards lived in Harlem.

Jan was the "Kortryck" who owned a Bouwery on Staten Island in 1674. (N. Y. Col. Mss., XXIII, 403). He spent part of his time at Harlem, but is last mentioned there Jan. 8th, 1677, when he is witness to a power of attorney, given by his old Schoonrewoerd friend, Jan Louwe Bogert.

His children were Cornelius, born 1645, Hendrick, 1648, Laurens, 1651, and Belitie, 1659, who was, as were the others, "uit Holland" and who married, December 8th, 1678, Jacob Jansen Decker, of Esopus, whither her brother Hendrick had gone to live.

Michiel Bastiaensen, who came in 1663, with his wife and children, the first four born in the town of Schoonrewoerd, in Gelderland, Holland, lived several years at Harlem, but on May 1st, 1669, leased a farm from John Archer, at Fordham, for five years, and on Jan. 1st, 1675, with his son-in-law, Hendrick Kiersen, hired from the widow Tourneur her farm upon Jochim Pieters and Van Keulens Hook, with house, barn, orchard, meadows, stock and tools, for three years from May 1st, ensuing.

On Oct. 26th, 1677, they leased 74 acres of land at Spuyten Duyvel from Jan Dyckman and Jan Nagel, for a term of twelve years, agreeing to pay each a hen for the first seven years, 150 guilders for the next three years, and for the last two years, 200 guilders.

This was the first successful effort to make improvements in that section of Manhattan Island, on which there was not another white man's hearthstone north of Harlem village.

In October 1673, he was elected a magistrate at Fordham, and was on the roll of the Night Watch at Harlem, as well as being identified with the Dutch church there.

His children were Reyer, born 1653; Metje, 1655, married Hendrick Kiersen; Annetie, 1658, married John Odell (ancestor of the Fordham Odells); Bastiaen, 1662; and Aefie, 1665, born in New York, who married Jacques Tourneur.

HARLEM

The pioneer settlers of Harlem were Henry and Isaac De Forest, French Huguenots, who came from Leyden, Holland, in 1636, choosing for their home the rich flat lands called Muscoota, about eight miles north of New Amsterdam, on Manhattan Island, where Henry obtained from director Van Twiller a grant of about 200 acres.

Here they built a farm house, in the rural Dutch style, forty two feet long and eighteen feet wide, surrounded by a high close fence of heavy round pickets, as a protection from the Indians, who eyed with ill-disguised suspicion this inroad upon their ancient hunting grounds.

The following spring they were cheered by the arrival of Dr. Johannes La Montagne, with his family, he having married Rachel, a sister of the De Forests.

Soon after, other settlers came, but the founders of Harlem were neither exclusively nor mainly Hollanders, as has been the common opinion. The community was made up mainly and in about even proportions of Hollanders and French Huguenots, while from the fir-clad hills of old Scandinavia, came sturdy Danes, Norwegians and Swedes, in faith Lutherans, inured to the soil, few in numbers, yet including several of undoubted worth and attainments.

Other exceptions there were, while all were men of probity, who had sacrificed much for liberty and the Reformed religion, and were equal to those of their times in intelligence, education and enterprise.

Highly industrious, they scorned, even in poverty, any dependence upon the charitable, while they could practice an honest trade or handicraft, such as each invariably possessed.

Their record, though not faultless, sustains this general good character; tried men, used to conquering difficulties, undaunted by the perils incident to a wild, a hostile land, theirs was the work of constructing a new society, a civilization, to which despotic Europe, then a stranger, could not tolerate.

Its safeguards—the church, the school, the civic magistracy, they were careful to bring with them, to plant and nurture as on a more congenial soil, and which, deeply rooted, still yield for us their golden fruits.

On September 15th, 1655, sixty-four canoes of armed savages landed at New Amsterdam, and began to break into the houses for plunder. All was alarm and confusion, Governor Stuyvesant being absent on an ex-

pedition to the Delaware with most of the garrison, and the enraged
Indians began a slaughter of the settlers, full fifty of whom fell in three
days, while over a hundred, mostly women and children, were carried
into captivity.

Hordes of armed savages, thirsting for blood, swept over the flat
at Harlem, slaying the settlers, plundering and burning their homes, and
devastating their bouweries. The Indians had threatened to root out the
Dutch, and kept their word, nor did they spare the English either, and
the history of these flats up to this period presented but a series of adversi-
ties, so it was considered time to arrest single-handed attempts to plant
bouweries, costing as they had so many valuable lives.

An interesting period is that which gave origin to the village of Harlem, which section was to be peopled and cultivated, but by some new and
more efficient mode than that already tried, and the Government had another object in view than that of promoting the settlement of this district.
This was to enhance the safety of New Amsterdam, as would result from
planting a strong village with a garrison, on this frontier end of the
island.

On March 4th, 1658, the Director General and Council of New
Netherland resolved to form a new village, and ground was broken for
the new settlement on August 14th, ensuing, hilarity and good cheer
marking the occasion. With its new advent into life and activity, the
infant settlement was called Nieuw Haerlem, from that famous city of
North Holland.

Soon several buildings were erected in the new village, and the settlers,
having steadily increased in numbers, now deemed themselves entitled to
a court of Justice, nominating a number of the best qualified persons to
rule as Magistrates, submitting their names to the Director and Council,
who confirmed three, they assuming their duties on August 16th, 1660.

Some of the inhabitants, in want of servants and laborers, bought a
number of negro slaves, sold at auction in Ft. Amsterdam, May 29th,
1664, they having arrived a few days before in the ship Sparrow, from
Curacao, these probably being the first slaves owned at Harlem.

An English fleet appeared suddenly before Fort Amsterdam, under
Col. Richard Nichols, and made an easy conquest of the province.

The Fort was surrendered on Sept. 8th, 1664, and the city, as also
the province, named New York. The wise and conciliatory course taken
by the new governor, Nichols, could not at once allay the feeling of indig-
nation which found expression among the Harlem people, or repair the
injury inflicted on the whole colony.

On the 11th of October, 1667, Governor Nichols gave the people of Harlem a patent, ample in its terms, which confirmed the titles of the owners, and determined and settled their landed rights.

The Holland and Zeeland fleets recaptured the fort at New York, on August 10th, 1673, in the name of the United Netherlands, naming the fort, "Willem Hendrick" and the City, "New Orange."

This political event was in the highest degree pleasing to the Harlem community, promising to its simple Belgian character and customs a happy perpetuity, while it restored, fresh and intact, the memories of the Fatherland. However, the rule of the Dutch was of short duration, for on the 10th of November, 1674, the fort was yielded up to the English Governor, Sir Edmund Andros, re-named Fort James, the city, New York, and the English form of government was restored. By its order to the town, December 7th, nominations were made to fill the places of constable and overseers, the new Schout (sheriff) being David des Marest, Cornelis Jansen Kortright took his seat as an overseer, and with him, Oblinus, Dyckman and Meyer.

A matter of great importance to the freeholders was a renewal or confirmation of the town patent, granted by former Governor Nichols; its confirmation now deemed imperative to preserve and secure these valuable franchises to them, their heirs or successors, so a new patent was drawn up, approved in Council, and signed by Governor Thomas Dongan, March 7th, 1686, the Patentees named being John Delaval, Resolved Waldron, Joost Van Oblinus, Daniel Tourneur, Adolph Mayer, John Spragge, Jan Hendrick Breevort, Jan Delamater, Barent Waldron, Isaac Delamater, Johannes Vermilje, Lawrence Jansen (Kortright), Peter Van Oblinus, Jan Dyckman, Jan Nagel, Arent Harmense Bussing, Cornelis Jansen (Kortright), Hester Delamater, Jacqueline Tourneur, Johannes Verveelen, William Haldron, Abraham Montagne and Pieter Parmentier.

No mention of a church edifice, or any effort to erect one here occurs until 1664, although Domine Michiel Zyperus, who came in 1660, a licientiate, who could preach and teach, but not perform the marriage ceremony, administer the sacraments, or admit to church membership, caused the flock at Harlem to resort to Stuyvesant's Bouwery, where Rev. Henry Selyns had been installed pastor, many having been received as members there, or in the church of Brooklyn, several miles away.

Domine Zyperus having departed, the religious interests suffering, and the congregation being unable to support a minister, Jan La Montagne was selected to fill the office of "Voorleser", or parish clerk, his duties being to lead in singing, read a sermon from some orthodox Dutch divine, comfort the sick, perform the burial service, instruct the children, and to these were usually added the duties of public auctioneer. Thereafter, the church had a regular succession of Voorlesers, to perform the various duties named.

At a feast given by the magistrates to Governor Stuyvesant, Jan. 23rd, 1665, in the new church which had been recently erected, the people sought counsel of their honored guest before he should leave for Holland, his advice being greatly leaned upon and valued.

This church, serving for a school-house also, was built on the north side of the Great Way, (since the Church Lane), on a vacant lot reserved for this purpose, and in 1680, measures were taken to build a new church, the old one being no longer adapted to the needs and improved tastes of the community, though still answering for a school.

The church was built of stone, upon a new site, Laurens Kortright and the Delamater family giving up their two north erven for this purpose.

It was thirty-six Dutch feet square, with a small steeple, and covered with shingles, and when completed, there came a proud moment for the villagers; it was when the gilded "haen", or weather cock, with the cap on which it perched, was raised to its lofty position on the tip of the steeple.

On September 30th, 1686, Domine Henry Selyns preached the first sermon in the new church, administered the Lord's Supper, and a liberal collection, twenty-two florins, was taken up.

Before the people separated, they nominated new town officers, who were Jan Van Brevoort, constable, and Jan Dyckman, Lawrence Jansen Kortright, and Isaac Delamater, magistrates, who were sworn in at New York, November 2nd, 1686.

It was three fourths of a century after the new church was built before the congregation secured a pastor to live among them, but the ministry of Domine Selyns, who preached frequently, seems to have gone smoothly, till the breaking out of the Leisler troubles in 1689, when several old members died, among them, Cornelis Jansen Kortright.

The Sunday services were kept up without interruption, under the lead of Guiliaem Bertholf, and the other voorlesers who succeeded him, and finally, in 1765, the church called Rev. Martinus Schoonmaker, who took up his residence at Harlem.

The court records, valuable as an index of the public morals, show that cases of trespass, slander and breach of the peace were too common, but that not a single manslaughter, action for divorce, a clear case of larceny or other serious crime is reported for the entire period under review. The inhabitants, wedded to plain and primitive habits, preserved all their characteristics in their ways and modes of living. Their houses began to be constructed with regard to permanence and even to style, being built of stone, of ample dimensions, though of only one full story. The low ceilings exposed heavy oak beams, often planed and beaded, and taste sometimes demanded wainscoting, either plain or in panels, around the rooms and hall, and up the broad stairway, with its oaken balustrades, leading to the loft.

The panes in the windows were about seven by nine inches, often set in leaden cross-bars, and protected by close strong shutters.

The fireplace, with usually no jambs, supported by the walls, gave ample room for all about the fire, and thus suspended, the chimney mouth opened wide, to catch the sparks and smoke, forming a convenient place in the proper season, to hang up hams, sausage and beef.

No people could have been more independent than the farmer, who burnt his own lime, made all the boots and shoes for the family, did most of his own carpenter work, while their help in the heavy farm work was mainly African slaves, numbering one to four whites.

The children were brought up to habits of industry, the sons invariably given a trade, and the daughters well taught in all household duties, while she who could not show her stores of domestic linens and other products of her maidenly skill, was considered but a poor candidate for matrimony. As soon as the flax and wool could be prepared in the fall, the women brought out the spinning wheel and made "homespun", as it was termed, to supply the family with clothing.

The carpet, when first introduced called in derision a dirt cover, was unknown here in those days. The bare floors, as scrupulously clean as the bare table on which they ate their food, was scrubbed, sprinkled with fine beach sand, and swept in waves or other figures, a sample of the general tidiness which ruled the premises.

Living so largely within themselves, they knew little of the dangers and diseases incident to luxury and indolence, and their pride was of a kind that was no bar to pleasure, if their only coach *was* a common wagon, or perchance an ox-cart, while their home-made linsey-woolsey gave content equally with the finest imported fabrics.

They were sociable, their tables being as free to their neighbors as to themselves, and hospitality could not do too much for the guest it welcomed, while their doors were wide open to let charity in and out, either to assist each other or relieve a stranger.

Intermarriages among the resident families was the rule, and he was thought a bold swain who ventured beyond the pale of the community to woo a mate, but an unaffected welcome awaited the blushing bride on her first arrival from the charming vales of Bloomingdale, the hills of Westchester, or rural home at Bergen, Hackensack or Esopus.

Large productive farms and a convenient market for all they had to sell, led to certain wealth, and no thriftier farmers were to be found anywhere. They were proud, too, of their broad acres, fine stock, lands well tilled and barns well filled, but nothing could win them to the display and ceremony of city life; though the latter, simplicity itself as compared with the demands of modern fashion, sets in stronger contrast the unpretentious yet rational style of living, which obtained in even the wealthier families. English modes and manners could make but slow advance among a people so tenacious of the Holland tongue, who for half a century kept their records in Dutch, and their accounts in guilders and stivers.

ESOPUS AND MINISINK

Esopus was originally a general name for the large and indefinite tract of country in which Wiltwick, now Kingston, (Ulster Co., N. Y.) is situated, and the name was subsequently applied, in a popular way, to Kingston itself, which was settled by the Dutch and French prior to 1657. In the spring of 1661, Gov. Peter Stuyvesant "Observing the situation and condition of the place called 'Esopus', and pleased thereat, erected our place into a village, and honored it with the name of Wiltwick."

The deed from the Indians to Thomas Chambers, who was one of the leading men there, was dated June 5, 1652, and on the 15th of April, 1660, Robert Swartwout was appointed the first "Schout," and Evert Pels, Cornelise·Barentse Shlect and Albert Heymans Roosa, the first "Schepens."

The old Dutch Church was organized on August 17th, 1659, when Hermanus Blom, whom Gov. Stuyvesant had sent to be Pastor there, preached two sermons, which were gratefully received by the settlers.

He served until 1668, and thereafter the Church had a regular succession of Pastors, among whom were Laurentius Van Gaasbeeck, Johannes Petrus Nucella, Georgius Wilhelm Mancius, and Domine Petrus Vas, the latter serving from 1710 to 1756, and greatly beloved by his people.

MOMBACCUS was the name of the general tract of country now embraced, in whole or in part, in the town of Rochester, Ulster County.

This tract was not called Rochester until early in the 18th century, after which the name of Mombaccus was applied, as it now is, to a small locality in the same town.

MINISINK is the name originally applied to a mining settlement by the Dutch and Swedes, on both banks of the Delaware River, prior to 1700, extending from the Water Gap, in a northerly direction about 40 miles. The Minisink region included a considerable portion of western and northern New Jersey, and the southerly sections of Orange and Sullivan counties, in the state of New York, as they now exist and part of the counties of Pike, Monroe and Northampton, in Pennsylvania.

The village of Minisink was situated in New Jersey, near the confluence of the Delaware and Neversink rivers.

There is a township in Orange County named Minisink, organized in 1780, which originally comprised a large area extending to the New Jersey line, but now considerably smaller.

The "Minisink" patent, granted by the Crown in 1704, covered a considerable portion of the Minisink country, and was so general and indefinite as to its boundaries, that for a long time it was a disturbing element among the inhabitants, owing to other grants of land about the same time.

The "Wawayanda" patent was granted in 1703, and the settlers of these patents had serious conflicts with the people of New Jersey, growing out of the uncertain boundary line of New York and New Jersey.

No action could be taken or maintained by either party, many hard and personal struggles took place to gain possession of the lands in question, and a lawless violence reigned over the disputed territory for more than three-quarters of a century, but the dispute was finally settled in 1767, by dividing the territory equally, or as nearly so as possible.

The Minisink was settled largely by Holland Dutch, who strayed down from Esopus, Mombaccus, Rochester, Marbletown and other places in Ulster County, whose descendants remained on the premises of their forefathers until after the Revolution.

At an early day, the people along the Delaware and Neversink Rivers, in the Minisink region, for a distance of forty miles, having a desire to hear the Gospel preached, concluded to form four congregations and to support one Minister. As there was no one to officiate in that capacity, and the people being generally from Holland, and of the Dutch Reformed Church, sent a young man, John Casperus Freyenmuth, to Holland, there to educate himself for the Ministry.

He went, finished his studies, was ordained, and became Minister of the four churches or congregations in 1741. He was agreeable to the people and gratefully remembered, his services continuing until 1755, when the French and Indian war started. In 1764, the Rev. Thomas Romeyn (Romaine) became Minister, his services continuing for several years, with satisfaction to himself, as well as to the people.

The Register of the Reformed Church at Machackemeck (Deerpark) shows that this church began services August 19, 1716, the Pastor on this occasion being Domine Petrus Vas, who lived in Kingston, and who often thereafter officiated. This church was in Deerpark, about a mile south of Port Jervis, near the junction of the Delaware and Neversink Rivers, and was burned during the Revolution, but on the same spot a new church was built.

The Walpeck Congregation was the name of the ancient church at a town formerly termed Walpeck, in Sussex County, New Jersey, a few miles south of Deerpark, and the register of this church shows services began there in 1741, under the ministry of John Casperus Freyenmuth.

The Smithfield Church was at Smithfield, Monroe Co., Pa., about ten miles from the Walpeck Church, while the Minisink Church, at Minisink, was situated eight miles south-west of the Machackemeck Church, in Montague township, near the line.

These were the four churches mentioned, all within a few miles of one another, and whose records have preserved much of interest pertaining to the early settlers.

The whole Minisink country was repeatedly raided by Indians during the Revolution, many of the settlers being killed and much property destroyed, and in 1778 and 1779, Brant's Indians swept through the Rondout and Neversink Valleys, with torch and gun, leaving death and destruction in their path.

"With Brant and Butler and their savages and tories on one hand, and British hosts on the other, the little town of Minisink and surrounding hamlets suffered all the horrors of a most bitter war.

The friends of today became the foes of tomorrow, and massacre of the settlers was of frequent occurrence. Scattered embers and smoking ruins in this and that little clearing amid the forests along the Delaware, Mohawk and Neversink, told where yesterday had stood the log-built homes of the pioneers, their crops and stock destroyed.

Patriot fathers fought unequal battles against lurking Indian or more treacherous Tory, while patriotic mothers, guarding their little ones, fled in terror here and there, hiding in the woods, with berries and herbs for food, the forest wilds their only shelter from the elements and foes alike.

Many women and children, refugees from the Wyoming Valley, perished from fatigue in trying to cross a swamp, known as the "Shades of death", while several children were born in that fearful spot, only to die there with their unhappy mothers.

Many there were who met death in massacre and battle, from ambush and open field, as on July 3d, 1778, at Wyoming, November 11th, same year, at Cherry Valley, and in July, 1779, the battle of Minisink, in which the town and near settlements were destroyed.

In the early autumn of 1779, General Sullivan and General James Clinton, with five thousand men, conducted an expedition in two divisions, one going west from Minisink, the other north-west of the Mohawk to Canajoharie, when it turned to the south-west along the Susquehanna.

The two columns met at Tioga Point, and on August 29th, 1779, routed 1,500 Tories and Indians, under Johnson, Butler and Brant, the battle taking place at Newton, now Elmira."

THE COURTRIGHT (KORTRIGHT) FAMILY

Bastiaen Van Kortryk, a native of the city of Kortryk, West Flanders, Belgium, emigrated to Holland about 1615, settling in the town of Leerdam, as has been shown. He had sons Jan and Michiel.

FIRST GENERATION IN AMERICA.

+1 Jan Bastiaensen (Van Kortryk), born 1618, at Leerdam, Holland, went to the town of Beest, not far from Leerdam, where he married and where his children were born, these being Cornelis, Hendrick, Laurens and Belitie. With his brother Michiel and their families, he sailed for New Amsterdam, embarking in the *Spotted Cow* April 16th, 1663, and had a Bouwery on Staten Island, but probably spent a part of his time at Harlem.

+2 Michiel Bastiaensen (Van Kortryk), born 1620, at Leerdam, also married and removed to the village of Schoonrewoert, not far from Leerdam, where his children, Reyer, Metje, Annetie and Bastiaen were born, his fifth child, Aefie, born in Harlem. They all came in the *Spotted Cow* in 1663, with Jan and his family, and soon came to Harlem, later making their home at Fordham.

SECOND GENERATION.

1 JAN BASTIAENSEN (VAN KORTRYK). ISSUE:

+3 Cornelis Jansen (Kortright), whose descendants composed the principal part of the late Kortright family of Harlem, was born at Beest, in Gelderland, Holland, in 1645, came out with his father, Jan Bastiaensen, in 1663, and in 1665, married Metje, daughter of Bastiaen Eleyessen, and the widow of Claes Teunisz Van Appeldorn, a lady who, after Jansen's early death in 1689, proved her ability both to manage his business and enhance his estate, the use of which, under his will dated Feb. 25, of said year, (but not proved till March 18th, 1706), she was to enjoy till her death or re-marriage.

Having been a trooper, he gave his eldest son Johannes, "the best horse, and the best saddle, and the best boots, and the best pistols, and holsters, and carbines and cutlass." He also left him, over and above his share of the estate, "the lot of land at Jochem Pieters, to wit;—the lot by the great gate."

A notable transaction was Nicholas de Meyer's sale Sept. 25th, 1669, of the two farms embraced in his patent, to the brothers Cornelis and Laurens Jansen, the first of whom being the ancestor of the Kortright family, or that branch afterwards known for its large landed possessions, of which this purchase formed the nucleus.

The removal of Verveelen having left the village (Harlem) without an ordinary keeper, Cornelis Jansen Kortright, who was well liked in the town, and afterwards enjoyed various public trusts, was admitted June 2d, 1670, to keep the ordinary on the usual conditions—to make suitable provisions for travellers, and not to sell any liquor to the Indians; he thereupon accepted the oath.

Cornelis and Laurens Jansen, having for a year worked the farm bought in partnership of Mr. De Meyer, agreed to part, as Laurens was about to lease the farm of Lubbert Gerritsen. The parties met for the purpose, Oct. 24th, 1670, and contracts were partly drawn, when they failed to agree. Cornelis having taken the De Meyer farm, Laurens on May 5th, 1671, gave him a lease of his part for four years, at the yearly rental of 400 guilders in grain. Their father, Jan Bastiaensen, and Bastiaen Eleyessen, the father-in-law of Cornelis, were present and subscribed this agreement. Laurens went to Esopus and married, and is not found at Harlem for several years.

Cornelis Jansen Kortright was constable in 1672, overseer in 1674, and 1681, and commissioner of the town court Feb. 2d, 1686 and Nov. 1st, 1687. On November 7th, 1673, by a majority of votes cast by the town, he was chosen and confirmed Captain of the Night Watch, consisting of four companies or corporalships, as some of the English exasperated at the recovery of the country by the Dutch, began to make trouble. He with others, was admitted to church membership at New Amsterdam, March 1st, 1673, and was a liberal supporter thereof.

On Feb. 6th, 1675, the Jansens, Cornelis and Laurens, completed a division of the lands bought of De Meyer, Cornelis taking the farm on Montagne's Flat, lots 18, Jochem Pieters, and 15, Van Keulen's Hook, and the two out-gardens.

Laurens took lot 2, Jochem Pieter's and lot 6, Van Kuelen's Hook, with the two erven, and also the orchard occupying two north gardens.

Laurens part being of most value, as it included the buildings, he agrees to give his brother 600 guilders. This property, as thus divided, composed the beginnings, respectively, of the Kortright and Low estates.

An event locally interesting was Cornelis Jansen's removal to his land on Montagne's Flat, since known as the Nutter Farm. On April 30th, 1684, he engaged Adrianus Westerhout to build him a house there, 22 by 36 feet, to be ready in six weeks, for which he agreed to pay 800 guilders in fat cattle, wheat and rye. Here Jansen established the famous tavern and stopping place, commonly called the Half-way House, and which continued to be kept after his death in 1689, by his widow.

It stood on the west side of Harlem Lane, at the foot of the hill about 109th Street. A little above this site, Valentine Nutter, on getting possession of the Kortright farm after the Revolution, built a new residence, which remained till swept away by the opening of 6th Avenue, on which it stood, its north corner touching 110th Street.

On March 7th, 1686, Thomas Dongan, Captain-General and Governor of the Province of New York, granted a patent to the proprietors which confirmed the patent granted by the former Governor, Richard Nichols, October 11th, 1667. On the list of patentees are named Cornelis and Laurens Jansen (Kortright), whose valuable franchises were secured to them, their heirs and successors, by the Dongan Patent, as it was professedly designed for quieting the freeholders and inhabitants in their ancient rights and privileges.

The widow, from her husband, is usually called Metje Cornelis, once Metje Jansen, and sometimes, from her father, Metje Bastiaens.

As the lists show, she drew largely of the common lands in the Flat; in the deed dated March 21, 1701, "bounded by a line leading from the southwest corner of the kitchen as the fence runs, to a small brook till it meets with the old lots of Cornelis Kortright, deceased."

In 1715, her family held 246 acres, of which Laurens Cornelissen held exclusively 77, and he and the other heirs jointly 169, which from 1715 to 1726, stood in the name of "Metje Cornelis' heirs."

The children of Cornelis Jansen and Metje (Bastiaens) Kortright were Aefie, Johannes, Annetie, Maria and Laurens, all of whom were called Cornelissen.

+4   Hendrick Jansen (Kortright), came with his father, Jan, in 1663 and bought land near Stuyvesant's Bouwery, Feb. 12th, 1669, but did not long hold it. He first styled himself Van Beest, but later in life from his father's birth place, was called Hendrick Jansen Van Kortright, and in the church records, his name was usually written Hendrick Jansen.

He and his brother Laurens, going to Esopus, both married there, Hendrick, on Dec. 14, 1672, to Catharine Hansen, "born in New York." She was probably a daughter of Hans Webber, "master at arms," who died in 1649, and whose widow, Elsje Pieters van Hamburg, married in 1650, Matthys Capido, removed to Esopus, and was killed by the Indians in 1663. On Sept. 28th, 1647, Hans Webber was appointed Captain at arms to the garrison at Fort Amsterdam, and on Sept. 1st, 1749, he was given power of attorney, by Anthony Barmoede, a Spaniard, to receive his share of thè prize Tobasco.

Hendrick's first child being born at Harlem, in 1674, he was probably then living there, but as before stated, he settled in Ulster County, buying land at Mombackus, town of Rochester, where he raised a large family who bore the name of Kortright or Cortright, and whose descendants have become numerous and widely scattered.

Hendrick lost his wife in 1740, and he died in 1741, aged 93., their children being Jan, Hendrick, Cornelis, Geertje, Arie, Antje, Laurens, Jacob, Jannetje, Peter, and Cathryn.

John, Cornelis, Lawrence and Peter Cortright subscribe for the minister at Rochester in 1717, and were leading men there.

+5   Laurens Jansen (Kortright), b. 1651, at Beest, Gelderland, Holland, and ancestor of the LOW family of Harlem, was the youngest son of Jan Bastiaensen (Van Kortryk), and came in 1663, with his parents.

He married in 1672, Mary, dau. of Albert Heymans Roosa, and his wife, Wyntje Ariens, at Esopus. The Roosa family came from Herwynen, Gelderland, Holland, sailing in the Bonte-koe, April 15th, 1660, and went immediately to Esopus, where he and his wife united with the church of which two years after, he became an elder.

Governor Stuyvesant giving a name to Wiltwick (Esopus), May 16th, 1661, appointed Roosa one of its first schepens. Here he took up land, for which he got a patent in 1664, and died in 1679, leaving a good estate, and eight surviving children.

Laurens Jansen's share of the De Meyer lands, bought jointly with his brother Cornelis, laid the foundation of the ample estate he acquired at Harlem, but which, with his grandsons, passed out of the name.

His election as an overseer in 1677, and repeatedly afterward, and the other responsible duties intrusted to him, evince the respect in which he was held. He died in 1727, probably at Harlem.

His name was usually written in the church records as Louwerens Jansen, and following the established Dutch custom of the time, his children were called Louwe, afterward shortened to Low, which was adopted as the family name, by his children, and not the name of Kortright, which most of the other descendants did.

His children were Annetie, Albert, Wyntie, Neeltie, John, Gysbert. Cornelis, Belitie, and Lawrence.

   6 Belitie (Isabella or Arabella) Jans was the youngest child and only daughter of Jan Bastiaensen, coming with her parents to Harlem in 1663, but as before stated, she, with her brother Hendrick removed to Esopus, where she m. Dec. 8th, 1678, Jacob Jansen Decker, she being 19 years of age, having been born in 1651.

They had a large family of children, whose descendants were very numerous, and now scattered widely.

   2 MICHIEL BASTIAENSEN (VAN KORTRIGHT), issue:

+7 Reyer Michielsen, eldest son of Michiel Bastiaensen, was b. at Schoonrewoerd, Holland, in 1653, coming in 1663 with his parents; he m. April 15, 1686, Jacomyntje, dau. of Jan Tibout, settling at Fordham, where he took part in building the church, of which he was an active member.

"A mortgage given by John Archer to Cornelis Steenwyck, of New York, in 1676, gave him full title and possession of the Manor of Fordham, which passed under his will and by certain deeds, to the Dutch church of New York. In getting possession, the church met with great opposition from the town of Westchester. This led in 1688 to a forcible entry by the officers and friends of the church. Elijah Barton, engaged with his father, Roger Barton, to keep possession for and in behalf of the town of Westchester, when on July 16th, in the afternoon, there came a great company of men with Nicholas Bayard, of New York, demanding admittance.

This being refused, Reyer Michiels and Teunis De Key, at Bayard's word, broke open the door and the Bartons were ousted and roughly handled.

With Bayard were also Nicholas Stuyvesant, Johannes Kip, Isaac Van Vleeck, Michiel Bastiaens and his wife, and sons Bastiaen, Reyer, Michiel, Hendrick Kiersen, and Jacques Tourneur. Also, "in the exployt" was Hannah (or Anna) Odell.

The Westchester authorities issued a warrant July 20th, "to take the bodies of the said Reyer Michiels, with the said complycetors", but the church maintained its hold and the lands were ultimately sold.

Reyer Michielsen died in 1733, having had children, Michiel, Reyer, Hendrick, Teunis, Hannah, Mary, Sarah, Jane, Jacomyntie, Johannes, some of whom being called Michiels and others Reyers.

8 Metje Michiels, b. in Holland, 1655, m. May 16, 1673, Hendrick Kiersen, son of Kier Wolters, and lived at Fordham.

9 Annetie Michiels, b. in Holland, in 1658, m. John Odell, who was the ancestor of the Fordham Odells.

+10 Bastiaen Michielsen, always so styled in the town books though in the church records usually called Bastiaen Kortright, came in 1663, with his parents, who lived at Harlem, afterward at Fordham.

He was born at Schoonrewoerd in 1662, the second son of Michiel Bastiaensen, and did not remove to Fordham as did the others, but remained at Harlem, where on March 28th, 1689, he married Jolante, daughter of John and Maria (Vermilye) La Montagne.

On Sept. 19th, 1701, he bought from Peter Van Oblinus a tract of land at Sherman's Creek, laid out in 1691, as lot No. 20.

This became the well-known Kortright farm, which continued in the family till 1786, consisting of forty-five acres and twenty perches.

Here Bastiaen Michielsen Kortright built and lived till very aged, at least his name in the tax list runs down to 1753. He also was the owner of two pieces of meadow at Kingbridge, the town giving him a deed Jan. 4th, 1700.

His children were Michael, Johannes, Aefie and Rachel.

11 Aefie Michiels, youngest child of Michiel Bastiaensen, was b. at Harlem in 1665, and m. June 17, 1683, Jacques Tourneur, son of Daniel and Jacqueline Tourneur. They resided at Fordham.

THIRD GENERATION.

3 CORNELIS JANSEN AND METJE (BASTIAENS) KORTRIGHT,
issue:

+12 Johannes Cornelissen, bap. April 24, 1673, m. May 26, 1701, Wyntie, dau. of Cornelis and Jannetie (Claessen) Dyckman, and d. in 1711, and in 1717, his widow m. Zacharias Sickels,

His children who bore the name of Kortright, were, Metje, Nicholas and Jannetie.

13 Aefie Cornelis, bap. May 30, 1666, m. Feb. 5, 1688, Jonas Lewis, and m. 2d, May 29, 1698, Marcus Tibout.

14 Annetie Cornelis, m. Aug. 27, 1701, Adrian Quackenbos.

15 Maria Cornelis, bap. April 2, 1679.

+16 Laurens Cornelissen, bap. Aug. 20, 1681, m. Oct. 22, 1703, Helena Benson, and m. 2d, 1708, Margaret Bussing, daughter of Arent

Bussing, and from Laurens sprang the main branch of the family at Harlem. He succeeded to the homestead on Harlem Lane, which at his death in 1726, fell in the division to his widow Grietie, together with other lands. He served as constable 1708-9.

His children by his first wife were Cornelis and Elizabeth, and by his second wife, Aaron, Lawrence, Eve, Susanna and Margaret.

4 HENDRICK JANSEN AND CATHARINE (HANSEN) CORTRIGHT, issue:

+17 Jan Hendricksen, bap. April 28, 1674, m. Nov. 3, 1700, Mary Van Vreedenburg, and 2d, about 1711, Elizabeth Van Kampen. He was b. at Harlem where his parents were living at the time, but came with them to Esopus where he was a farmer; he also lived at Rochester, Ulster County, N. Y., and with his brothers, was a prominent man there.

His children were Willem, Hendrick, Appolonia, and Arien, by his first wife, and by his second, Johannes and Maria.

+18 Hendrick, b. in 1677, m. Nov. 3, 1700, Mary de. Wit, and m. 2d, Dec. 6, 1703, Cathryn Crom, widow of Arie Van Etten. He also lived in Ulster County, where he was a farmer, and had children, Hendrick, Abraham, Catharina, Geertjen and Bastiaan.

+19 Cornelis Hendricksen, bap. in N. Y., Nov. 3, 1680, b. at Mombaccus, Ulster County, N. Y., m. Dec. 26, 1701, Christina Roosekrans.

He was a farmer in Ulster County, and removed to Marbletown, where most of his children were born, who were, Hendrick, Magdalena, Catrina, Johannes, Sara, Cornelis and Benjamin.

20 Annatie Hendricks (no record of baptism), m. Sept. 2, 1695, Jacob Decker, who resided at Mombaccus, Ulster County, N. Y.

21 Geertjen Hendricks, bap. July 23, 1682, m. April 23, 1714, Abraham Schut, widower of Heyltjen Dekker.

22 Arie Hendricksen, bap. May 18, 1684, no further record.

+23 Laurens Hendricksen, bap. June 24, 1688, m. Dec. 21, 1715, Sara ten Eyk, b. at Hurley. They removed to Wawarsing, Ulster County, where they became members of the church, and where many of their children were born, who were, Janneke, Cornelis, Matheus, Hendericus, Abraham, Jacobus, Sara, and Maria.

24 Jacob Hendricksen, bap. Oct. 16, 1692, no further record.

25 Jannetje Hendricks, bap. Nov. 18, 1694, m. June 12, 1717, Hendrick Decker, who lived in Ulster County.

+26 Pieter Hendricksen, bap. Jan. 4, 1697, died 1744, m. Jan. 9, 1717, Mary Van Garden, and had children, Hendrick, Rachel, Cathrina, Abraham, Tjetjen, Annetje, and possibly Marya and Petrus.

27 Cathryn Hendricks, bap. July 9, 1699, no further record.

5 LAURENS JANSEN AND MARY (ROOSA) KORTRIGHT, issue:

28 Annetie Low, bap. July 8, 1674, m. Gysbert Bogert.

+29 Albert Low, bap. Nov. 11, 1676, m. Oct. 2, 1702, Susanna Dela mater, daughter of John Delamater, and with his brother John, removed to Somerset County, New Jersey, served as a deacon at Raritan and d. in 1739, leaving his farm to his sons, Abraham and Cornelis. His children were Maria, John, Lawrence, Abraham and Cornelis.

30 Wyntie Low, bap. Apr. 23, 1679, no further record.

31 Neeltie Low, bap. May 20, 1682, m. May 27, 1703, Conrad Lamberts.

+32 John Low, bap. Apr. 29, 1685, m. June 20, 1707, Jannetje Corssen, removed to Somerset County, N. J., and had children, Lawrence, Gysbert, Benjamin, Cornelis, Maria, Wyntie, Mary and Teunis.

33 Gysbert Low, bap. Aug. 14, 1687, no further record.

+34 Cornelis Low, b. 1691, m. 1715, Judith Middagh, and had children Dirck, Mary, Cathelyn, Gysbert, Cornelis, Judith, John, Gerrit and Anna.

35 Belitie Low, bap. June 18, 1693, no further record.

+36 Lawrence Low, born in 1698, m. June 12, 1725, Jannetje, daughter of Marinus Roelofs van Vleckeren, of Bloomingdale. He succeeded to his father's lands at Harlem, which his brother Albert, as heir at law, released to him Dec. 8, 1731, and he also made several considerable other purchases. He made his will in 1754, which was proved Nov. 4, 1755, by which his widow was to enjoy his estate during her life, but ten years before her death, which was in 1772, her two sons made a formal division of the property, and sold some of it, whence it would appear they had acquired the interests of their mother and sister.

Their children were, Dinah, Marinus and John.

7 REYER AND JACOMYNTIE (TIBOUT) MICHIELSEN, issue:

+37 Michiel, m. (?)

38 Reyer.

39 Hendrick.

40 Teunis.
41 Hannah, m. Leonard Vincent.
42 Mary, m. Benjamin Haviland.
43 Sarah, bap. Jan. 30, 1689, m. Joseph Haviland.
44 Jane, bap. June 21, 1693, m. Benjamin Corsa, Apr. 17, 1718.
45 Jacomyntie, bap. Dec. 29, 1695.
46 Johannes, bap. Feb. 2, 1698.

The sons of Michiel, (being Reyer and Michael) retained the name of Michaels, but other of Reyer's sons took the patronymic Reyers. Hence have descended the two families of Westchester County, and other sections of New York, named Ryer, and Michael, or as also written, McKeel or Mekeel.

10 Bastiaen Michielsen and Jolante (La Montagne) Kortright, issue:

47 Michael, bap. Apr. 14, 1697.
+48 Johannes, bap. May 6, 1702, m. Aeltie Vermilye.
49 Aefie, m. John Devoor, Apr. 29, 1722.
50 Rachel, m. Isaac La Montagne.

FOURTH GENERATION.

12 Johannes and Wyntie (Dyckman) Kortright, issue:

51 Metje, bap. Feb. 27, 1702, m. Sept. 2, 1723, John Bussing.
+52 Nicholas, m. Feb. 5, 1731, Elizabeth Van Huyse, and 2d, Elizabeth Conteyn, widow of —— Peltrong, Apr. 15, 1738.
53 Jannetie, m. Sept. 2, 1723, Johannes Van Wyck.

On the death of his uncle Laurens, in 1726, the Kortright lands were divided, and Nicholas took as his portion 101 acres, and purchased other land, owning altogether 144 acres. He died Nov. 19, 1743.

16 Laurens and Helena (Benson) Kortright, issue:

+54 Cornelis, bap. May 30, 1704, m. Nov. 11, 1727, Hester Cannon.
55 Elizabeth, bap. Nov. 3, 1706, m. Apr. 19, 1753, Gilbert Garrison.

16 Laurens and Margaret (Bussing) Kortright, issue:

+56 Aaron, d. 1789, m. Margaret Delamater.
57 Lawrence, d. 1761, unm. His will dated Nov. 8, 1760.
58 Eve, m. 1732, Adolph Benson.
59 Susanna, m. 1735, Aaron Meyer.
60 Margaret, m. 1740, Abraham Meyer.

Cornelis Kortright (54), eldest son of Laurens Cornelissen Kortright, m. Hester, dau. of John Cannon, of New York, and owned property in Queen (now Pearl) Street, where he carried on the baking business.

He was assistant alderman of Montgomery Ward, 1738-40. His two slaves, implicated in the Negro Plot of 1741, were transported to San Domingo. After his death Apr. 15, 1745, his business was continued by his widow and son Cornelius.

Aaron Kortright (56), m. Margaret, dau. of John Delamater. He purchased the Delamater farm on Montagne's Flat, and accompanying lands, part of which he sold, and recovered by purchase the lower half of the Delamater farm, which embraced 12 acres east of the Lane, on which were the buildings, and 60 acres on the Flat, a portion being on the heights.

In 1762 and 1765, he gave liens on some of his lands bought of Delamater to his nephew, Lawrence Kortright, and finally the two made an exchange, Apr. 28, 1772, Lawrence taking the farm and woodlands, and giving Aaron and his wife a deed for 241 acres of the Wawayanda patent in Orange County, to go after their death to their sons, Lawrence, John and Aaron Kortright— whither they removed, and where their descendants are still found.

Lawrence Kortright (57), the last of the name to hold the homestead, died in 1761, unmarried. He had devised his estate to one Sarah Gilmore, wife of William Nutter, and afterward, Apr. 5, 1760, gave her a deed for the farm and two woodland lots. But by another will, of Nov. 8th, ensuing, he revokes, to quote his words, "a pretended last will and testament said to have been made by me in favor of Sarah Nutter, which last will and testament, (if any such there be), and also certain deeds of lease and release for my real estate, (if such there be), pretended to have been made and executed by me to her, I do declare, on the faith of a Christian, to have been obtained from me by fraud and circumvention, and without any valuable consideration received by me for the same."

By this second will, he divides his property among his kindred, and the Kortright heirs refusing to give up the premises, Valentine Nutter, only child and heir of Sarah, brought an ejectment suit in 1771; but after "divers difficulties, controversies and disputes about the said lands," a compromise was made, Aaron Kortright and his co-heirs, for a consideration, releasing their claims by deeds dated 1789 and 1799.

17 JAN AND MARY (VAN VREEDENBURG) KORTRIGHT, issue:

+61 Willem, bap. Aug. 4, 1701, m. Margriet Jansen.
62 Hendrick, bap. July 1, 1704, m. Gerritjen Van Bunchoten, Oct. 11, 1730.
63 Appolonia, bap. Aug. 11, 1706, m. Johannes Westfall.
+64 Arien, bap. Sept. 11, 1709, m. Elizabeth Cool.

17   JAN AND ELIZABETH (VAN KAMPEN) KORTRIGHT, issue:
65   Johannes, bap. May 25, 1712, m. Catharine Cortright, Aug. 27, 1745.
66   Maria, bap. Mar. 6, 1715, m. Jurian Tappan.

18   HENDRICK AND MARY (DE WITT) KORTRIGHT, issue:
67   Tjerck, bap. Mar. 9, 1701.

18   HENDRICK AND CATHARINE (CROM) KORTRIGHT, issue:
+68 Hendrick, bap. Mar. 17, 1706, m. Margriet Decker.
+69 Abram, bap. Nov. 17, 1706, m. Margriet Kuikendal.
70   Catharine, bap. Oct. 26, 1709, m. Teunis Middagh, Sept. 13, 1728.
71   Geertjen, bap. Dec. 7, 1712.
+72 Bastiaan, bap. June 24, 1716, m. Rachel Decker.

19   CORNELIS AND CHRISTINA (ROOSEKRANS) CORTRIGHT, issue:
+73 Hendrick, bap. Mar. 29, 1703, m. Jannetje Ennes, Nov. 6, 1724.
74   Magdalena, bap. Aug. 4, 1706, m. Benjamin Decker.
75   Catrina, bap. Mar. 25, 1711, m. Johannes Kortright, Aug. 27, 1745.
+76 Johannes, bap. Aug. 15, 1714, m. Margriet Dennemarken, Jan. 24, 1735.
77   Sara, bap. Aug. 2, 1719, m. Samuel Schammers (Chambers).
78   Cornelis, bap. June 17, 1722, m. Mary Schoonmaker, April, 1759.
+79 Benjamin, bap. Jan. 16, 1726, m. Arriantje Oosterhout, Oct. 2, 1759.

23   LAURENS AND SARAH (TEN EYCK) KORTRIGHT, issue:
80   Janneke, bap. May 18, 1718, m. Benjamin Hoornbeek, May 6, 1739.
81   Cornelis, bap. Nov. 20, 1720.
82   Matheus, bap. Nov. 20, 1720.
83   Hendericus, bap. Sept. 22, 1723.
+84 Abraham, bap. June 4, 1727, m. Jannetje Van Kampen, May 28, 1769.
+85 Jacobus, b. about 1731, m. Catrina De Puy.
86   Sara, bap. Sept. 29, 1734, m. Jan Kittel, Sept. 10, 1754.
87   Maria, bap. Jan. 17, 1756.

26. PIETER AND MARY (VAN GARDEN) KORTRIGHT, issue:
88   Hendrick, bap. Sept. 22, 1717, m. Elizabeth Hoornbeek, Dec. 28, 1739.
89   Rachel, bap. Jan. 10, 1720, m. Gysbert Van Garden.
90   Catrina, bap. Jan. 28, 1722, m. Abraham Van Camp, about 1742, and Jacobus Van Garden, Apr. 15, 1753.
+91 Abraham, bap. Oct. 18, 1724, m. Cornelia Bunschoten, Sept. 18, 1747, m. 2d, Rebecca Quick.
92   Tjaetjen, bap. Aug. 27, 1727, m. Cornelis Kortright, Dec. 6, 1747.

93   Annatje, bap. Feb. 10, 1734, m. Alexander Van Garden, May 6, 1750.

29. ALBERT AND SUSANNA (DELAMATER) LOW, issue:

94   Maria, bap. Sept. 15, 1703, m. Hendrick Pettinger.
95   John, bap. June 2, 1707.
96   Lawrence, bap. Oct. 25, 1710.
+97   Abraham, bap. Oct. 13, 1719, m. Ida Stoothoff, Jan. 23, 1753.
+98   Cornelis, bap. Oct. 13, 1719, m. Catrina Van Duyn, Sept. 27, 1746.

32. JOHN AND JANNETJE (CORSSEN) LOW, issue:

+99   Lawrence, bap. about 1711, m. Geertie Roosa.
100   Gysbert, bap. Oct. 9, 1714, m. Persella ——————.
+101   Benjamin, bap. Oct. 17, 1716, m. Neeltie Van Nest.
+102   Cornelis, bap. about 1718, m. Johanna Jansen.
103   Maria, bap. Apr. 4, 1719, m. Jan Cool, Mar. 19, 1749.
104   Wyntie, bap. Apr. 4, 1721.
105   Mary, bap. Aug. 18, 1723.
+106   Teunis, bap. Apr. 3, 1728, m. Mary Hall.

34. CORNELIS AND JUDITH (MIDDAGH) LOW, issue:

+107   Dirck, bap. Sept. 26, 1717, m. Rebecca Emmons, June 1, 1747.
108   Mary, bap. April 14, 1721, m. Abraham Bodine.
109   Cathelyn, bap. Mar. 3, 1723.
110   Gysbert, bap. Nov. 14, 1725.
+111   Cornelis, bap. Dec. 3, 1729, m. Annatje Dildein.
112   Judith, bap. Oct. 25, 1730, m. Johannes Van Nest.
+113   John, bap. Feb. 4, 1733, m. Catharina Emmons.
+114   Gerrit, bap. Aug. 3, 1735, m. Rachel ——————.
115   Anna, bap. Jan. 21, 1739, m. Abraham Van Vliet.

36 LAWRENCE AND JANNETJE (VAN VLECKEREN) LOW, issue:

116   Dinah, bap. Mar. 11, 1730, m. Jacobus Tourneur.
117   Marinus, m. Deborah Oblinus, Feb. 7, 1754.
+118   John, m. Bridget Meyer, June 22, 1765.

37 MICHIEL MICHAELS (NAME OF WIFE NOT RECOVERED), issue:

119   Reyer, m. Elizabeth Drake.
+120   Michael, m. Mazerie ——.

CORNELIS AND ELIZABETH (JACOBS) MICHAELS, issue:

121   Machtel, bap. Mar. 30, 1708.
122   Dina, bap. June 1, 1708.
123   Jannetje, bap. June 1, 1708.

48 JOHANNES AND AELTIE (VERMILYE) KORTRIGHT, issue:

124   John, m. Aefie Devoor, Dec. 25, 1774.

Johannes Bastiaens (48), as he is styled in certain deeds, but calling himself Johannes Michielsen Kortright, was a weaver but succeeded to the farm at Sherman's Creek, which he mortgaged in 1768, and soon after removed to New York. Having lost his wife, he died about 1775. His son John Courtright, as he wrote his name, married in 1774, his cousin, Aefie or Effie, daughter of John and Aefie Devoor, of Hoorn's Hook, and was the last of the family to own the ancestral farm, of which he made sale, May 24, 1786, to Cornelius Harsen, this being a part of the Ft. George Tract, which was parceled into lots and publicly sold Oct. 14, 1868.

FIFTH GENERATION

52 NICHOLAS AND ELIZABETH (VAN HUYSE) KORTRIGHT, issue:
125   John, b. 1732.

52   NICHOLAS AND ELIZABETH (CONTEYN) KORTRIGHT, issue:
126   Frances, bap. Oct. 4, 1741, m. John Norris.
+127   Nicholas, bap. Dec. 26, 1743, m. Elizabeth ——.

Nicholas (127), a sail maker, owned property in N. Y., where he lived, and was a vestryman of Trinity Church, 1787 to 1792. His wife Elizabeth died in 1789, aged 46 years, and he died in 1820.

54   CORNELIS AND HESTER (CANNON) KORTRIGHT, issue·
+128   Lawrence, bap. Nov. 27, 1728, m. Hannah Aspinwall, May 6, 1755.
129   John, bap. Jan. 3, 1731, m. Elizabeth Davenport.
130   Cornelis, bap. Dec. 17, 1732, d. at St. Croix, Feb. 1775.
131   Maria, bap. Oct. 3, 1736, m. John W. Hanson, Jan. 29, 1763.
132   Helena, bap. Apr. 18, 1739, m. Abraham Brasher, July 13, 1758.
133   Margaret, bap. Oct. 14, 1741.
134   Elizabeth, bap. June 30, 1745, m. William R. Van Cortlandt, Jan. 3, 1765.

56   AARON AND MARGRIET (DELAMATER) KORTRIGHT, issue:
135   Ann Elizabeth, m. Henry Sherman, May 15, 1766.
136   Eve, b. July 21, 1752, m. Caspar Writer, Sept. 8, 1772.
+137   Lawrence, b. Dec. 21, 1758, m. Mary Cox, June 4, 1782.
+138   Aaron, m. Heyltie Van Garden.
+139   John, m. Jannetie Middagh.
140   Susanna, m. —— Spinkstead.
141   Rebecca, m. Amasa Mathews, about 1774.

61   WILLIAM AND MARGRIET (JANSEN) KORTRIGHT, issue:
+142   Hendrick W., bap. May 19, 1736, m. Catrina Middagh.
+143   Elias, bap. May 30, 1738, m. Deborah Comstock.
144   Willem, bap. Oct. 31, 1739.

+145 Josias W., bap. Nov. 11, 1741, m. Cornelia Cool, Oct. 15, 1766.
 146 Daniel, bap. Apr. 23, 1744.
 147 Susanna, bap. Nov. 10, 1745, m. Hendrick Westfal.
 148 Gerretje, bap. July 17, 1748, m. Gideon Middagh, Nov. 30, 1766.

64 ARIE AND ELIZABETH (COOL) KORTRIGHT, issue:

+149 Johannes, bap. June 18, 1734, m. Susanna Kittel, Nov. 30, 1762.
 150 Elizabeth, bap. June 17, 1740, m. Derick Westfal.
 151 Cattrina, bap. May 3, 1743, m. Jurian Wintermout.
 152 Lydia, bap. Feb. 22, 1747, m. Samuel Williams, Apr. 20, 1769.
+153 Samuel, bap. Sept. 10, 1749, m. Margriet Westfael.

68 HENDRICK AND MARGRIET (DECKER) KORTRIGHT, issue:

 154 Elizabeth, bap. Jan. 10, 1734, m. Jan Middagh, Jan. 12, 1753.
+155 Salamon, bap. May 18, 1736, m. Cornelia Cool, Dec. 9, 1756.
 156 Lea, bap. May 31, 1738, m. Jacob I. De Witt, Mar. 30, 1759.
 157 Lydia,.bap. Sept. 19, 1740, m. Cornelius Van Garden.
+158 Daniel, bap. May 3, 1743, m. Antje Westbrock.
+159 Moses, bap. Mar. 24, 1745, m. Antje Van Etten.
 160 Femmetje, bap. Apr. 12, 1747.
 161 Sarah, bap. Nov. 26, 1749.
 162 Janneke, bap. Feb. 2, 1752, m. Joel Decker, Dec. 1, 1771.

69 ABRAHAM AND MARGRIET (KUIKENDAL) KORTRIGHT, issue:

 163 Elizabeth, bap. May 3, 1737.
 164 Femmetje, bap. May 3, 1737.

72 BASTIAAN AND RACHEL (DECKER) KORTRIGHT, issue:

 165 Rachel, bap. June 17, 1740, m. Leendert Brink, Dec. 14, 1764.
 166 Sara, bap. Jan. 6, 1745, m. Johnathan Middagh.
+167 Jonas, bap. Oct. 19, 1746, m. Elizabeth Davis.
 168 Catharina, bap. June 21, 1747, m. Benjamin Quick.
+169 Jacob, bap. Mar. 26, 1749, m. Femmetje Deenmark.
 170 Elizabeth, bap. June 24, 1752, m. Joseph Showers, June 1, 1775.
+171 Salomon, bap. Oct. 20, 1754, m. Anna Ayers.

PETRUS AND MARYA (WESTFAEL) KORTRIGHT, issue:

 172 Lydia, bap. July 7, 1755, m. Jacob Plough.
 173 Janneke, bap. Jan. 28, 1759, m. Samuel Quick, June 1, 1775.
 174 Arie, bap. Apr. 20, 1760.
+175 Symon, bap. July 20, 1764, m. Cathrina Ennes, June 20, 1784.
 176 Sophryn, bap. July 29, 1770.
 177 Antje, bap. Aug. 28, 1772, m. Isaac Swartwout.
 178 Jannetje, bap. Nov. 16, 1774.

73 HENDRICK AND JANNETJE (ENNES) CORTRIGHT, issue:

+179 Cornelis, bap. June 27, 1725, m. Tjaetje Kortright, Dec. 6, 1747,
      m. 2d Helena Rosekrantz, Apr. 8, 1750.

180   Catrina, bap. Feb. 12, 1727.
+181 Daniel, bap. Apr. 13, 1729, m. Russie Van Aken, Mar. 1, 1752.
+182 Benjamin, bap. about 1731, m. Catrina Hover, about 1762.
183   iJohannes, bap. May 19, 1736, unm.
+184 Willem E., bap. Oct. 31, 1739, m. Sarah Handshaw, Aug. 8, 1768.
+185 Abraham, bap. July 23, 1741, m. Neeltie Swartwout, about 1770.
186   Jenneke, bap. Jan. 13, 1745, m. Johannes Van De Merken.
+187 Jacobus, bap. Mar. 8, 1747, m. Anna Quick, m. 2d, Jannetje Van
      Aken.
188   Cornelia, bap. June 21, 1749, m. Henry Hover.

76 JOHANNES AND MARGRIET (DENNEMARKEN) CORTRIGHT,
issue:

+189 John, bap. Nov. 1, 1738, m. Mary, dau. of Dirck and Rachel (Van
      Keuren) Van Vliet.
+190 Christopher, bap. June 17, 1740, m. Martha Miller.
191   Samuel, bap. July 5, 1742.
+192 Elisha, bap. Jan. 13, 1745, m. Alida, (or Huldah) Dingman.
+193 Abraham V., bap. Oct. 2, 1748, m. Effie Drake.
194   Elizabeth, bap. Sept. 3, 1751, m. John Schoonhover.
195   Christina, bap. June 9, 1754.

79 BENJAMIN AND ARRIANTJE (OOSTERHOUT) KORTRIGHT,
issue:

+196 Lawrence, bap. Mar. 2, 1760, m. Maria Kortright.
197   Anna, bap. Aug. 16, 1765, m. Samuel Hoornbeek.
198   Sarah, bap. Apr. 25, 1768, m. Jacob Schoonmaker.
199   Janneke, bap. Dec. 9, 1770.
+200 Cornelius, bap. Jan. 1, 1775, m. Jemima Morris.
201   Maria, bap. Apr. 23, 1780.
202   Catherina, bap. Oct. 16, 1783, m. Jacob Vernoy.

Benjamin Kortright (79), resided at Pine Ridge, Ulster County, and several of his children were baptized at the Ref. Dutch Church at Wawarsing.

He received his commission as Captain in the 3d Regiment, Ulster County Militia, (organized at New Paltz) Oct. 25, 1775, under the command of Col. Levi Pawling, in the Revolutionary service.

He was the leader of the "Kortright" expedition, mentioned in Smith's legends of Shawangank, in which he pursued some Indians who had killed several of the settlers.

He evidently was prominent at Rochester, where he served as trustee from 1785 to 1802, town clerk, 1794 to 1804, school commissioner from 1797 to 1800, and also held other official positions. In his will, he mentions children, Cornelius, Annatie, Sarah, Jenekah, Maria, and Catharine and also grandsons, Benjamin Kortright and Benjamin Schoonmaker, Jr.

84 ABRAHAM AND JANNETJE (VAN KAMPEN) KORTRIGHT, issue:
203 Elsje, bap. July 22, 1770, m. Peter Burger.
204 Sara, bap. June 19, 1774, m. John Hunt.
+205 Hendrick, bap. June 21, 1777, m. Maria Oosterhout.

85 JACOBUS AND CATRINA (DE PUY) KORTRIGHT, issue:
206 Hendericus, bap. Sept. 2, 1759.
207 Maria, bap. July 19, 1763, m. Lawrence Kortright.
208 Catharina, bap. Oct. 16, 1765, m. Jacob Louw, Jan. 6, 1786.

**91 ABRAHAM PETER AND CORNELIA (BUNSCHOTEN)
KORTRIGHT, issue:**
209 Elizabeth, bap. Oct. 22, 1749, m. Abraham Quick.
+210 Hendrick, bap. Feb. 9, 1752, m. Cornelia Decker.
211 Antoni, bap. Mar. 3, 1754.

91 ABRAHAM PETER AND REBECCA (QUICK) KORTRIGHT, issue:
212 Annatie, bap. Jan. 16, 1763, m. Moses Brink, Mar. 11, 1787.
213 Rachel, bap. July 4, 1765, m. Benjamin Decker, Nov. 23, 1788.
+214 Isaac, bap. Dec. 7, 1767, m. Susanna Dailey.
215 Abraham, bap. Mar. 4, 1772, m. Blandina Courtright, Oct. 10, 1801.
216 Resyna, bap. May 23, 1783, m. Isaac Decker.

97 ABRAHAM AND IDA (STOOTHOF) LOW, issue:
217 Rem, bap. Jan. 20, 1754.
218 Abraham, bap. Apr. 10, 1757, m. Maria Garretsen.
219 Maria, bap. Aug. 10, 1760.
220 Catharina, bap. June 29, 1766.

98 CORNELIS AND CATRINA (VAN DUYN) LOW, issue:
221 Sarah, bap. July 26, 1751.
222 Cornelis, bap. Apr. 27, 1755.
223 Catrentie, bap. July 24, 1757.
224 William, bap. Mar. 23, 1774.
225 John, bap. Oct. 30, 1776.

99 LAWRENCE AND GEERTIE (ROOSA) LOW, issue:
226 John.
227 Gysbert.
228 Henry.
229 Jannetie.
230 Elizabeth.
231 Charity.
232 Lavina.

101 BENJAMIN AND NEELTIE (VAN NEST) LOW, issue:

233 Peter, bap. Nov. 6, 1743, m. Sarah ——, m. 2d, Hannah Ten Eyck.
234 John, bap. Mar. 23, 1746.
235 Janneke, bap. Mar. 31, 1748.
236 Cornelis, bap. May, 1750, m. Catlina Stryker.
237 Benjamin, bap. Dec. 26, 1757.
238 Gisbert, bap. Sept. 25, 1762.
239 Isaac, bap. June 29, 1766.

102 CORNELIS AND JOHANNA (JANSEN) LOW, issue:

240 John, bap. May 13, 1752.
241 Benjamin, bap. Oct. 28, 1753.

106 TEUNIS AND MARY (HALL) LOW, issue:

242 John, bap. Aug. 2, 1752.
243 Thomas, bap. Feb. 6, 1755.
244 Mary, bap. Mar. 21, 1756.

107 DIRCK AND REBECCA (EMMONS) LOW, issue:

245 Maria, b. Feb. 23, 1748, m. Joseph Carle.
246 Dirck, b. Nov. 27, 1749, m. Dorothea Ten Eyck.
247 Johannes, b. June 23, 1751, m. Sarah ——
248 Eunice, b. Jan. 4, 1753, m. —— Sutphen.
249 Catherine, b. Mar. 8, 1754, m. —— Kimberly.
250 Cornelius, b. Dec. 27, 1755.
251 Rebecca, b. Dec. 12, 1757, m. William Verbruyck.
252 Gisbert, b. Oct. 19, 1759, m. Margaret Emery.
253 Anna, b. Oct. 20, 1761, m. —— Hall.
254 Abraham, b. Sept. 10, 1765, m. Mrs. Stevens.
255 Jacob D., b. May 12, 1767, m. Martha Perlee, m. 2d, Martha Edgar, m. 3d, Francis Wilds.
256 Sarah, b. Jan. 15, 1769, m. Peter Stryker.
257 Isaac, b. Feb. 25, 1772, m. Elizabeth Hall, 2d, Jane Sutphen.

111 CORNELIS AND ANNATJE (DILDEIN) LOW, issue:

258 Cornelius, bap. Sept. 9, 1750.
259 Cathelyn, bap. Nov. 10, 1751.
260 Judick, bap. Sept. 8, 1754.
261 Gysbert, bap. Oct. 24, 1757.
262 Maria, bap. Mar. 4, 1759.
263 Rebecca, bap. June 21, 1761.

113 JOHN AND CATHARINE (EMMONS) LOW, issue:

264 Johannes, bap. May 22, 1757.
265 Abraham, bap. July 15, 1757.
266 Eunice, bap. Oct. 13, 1765.
267 Judick, bap. June 12, 1768.

114 GERRIT AND RACHEL (——) Low, issue:
268 Judith, bap. July 24, 1756.
269 Cornelius, bap. Feb. 12, 1758.
270 Sara, bap. Apr. 1, 1764.
271 Gysbert, bap. Feb. 16, 1766.
272 Abraham, bap. Aug. 7, 1768.

118 JOHN AND BRIDGET (MEYER) Low, issue:
273 Adolf, b. Apr. 30, 1771.
274 Sarah, b. Apr. 4, 1773.
275 Bridget, bap. Dec. 14, 1782.

120 MICHAEL AND MAZERIE (——) REYERS, issue:
276 Marytje, bap. Mar. 21, 1710.
277 Jacomyntje, bap. Mar. 21, 1711.
278 Michael, bap. Nov. 6, 1722, m. Elizabeth Vandervoor.
279 William.

SIXTH GENERATION.

127 NICHOLAS AND ELIZABETH (——) KORTRIGHT, issue:
+280 James B., m. Elizabeth Warner, May 21, 1794.
 281 Nicholas.

128 LAWRENCE AND HANNAH (ASPINWALL) KORTRIGHT, issue:
+282 John, m. Catharine Seaman, May 2, 1793.
 283 Sarah, m. Col. John Heyliger, of Santa Cruz, in 1775.
 284 Elizabeth, m. Hon. James Monroe, later Pres. of the U. S., in 1786.
 285 Hester, m. Nicholas Gouverneur, Esq., in 1790.
 286 Mary, m. Thomas Knox, Esq., in 1793.

Lawrence Kortright (128), the eldest son of Cornelius, also a merchant, became wealthy and prominent. In the old French war he was part owner of several privateers fitted out at New York against the enemy. He was one of the founders of the Chamber of Commerce in 1768. He had a large interest in Tryon County lands, and on his purchase the township of Kortright was settled. He had identified himself with the Episcopal Church, and during the Revolution remained quiet at his residence, but his sympathies were with his country. His residence was 192 Queen Street about the time mentioned. In 1778, partly on his security, Judge Fell, then a prisoner in the Provost, obtained his release. He died in 1794, but before his death he conveyed his farm at Harlem with some woodland, to his only son, John.

137 LAWRENCE AND MARY (COX) KORTRIGHT, issue:

287 Lydia, b. July 25, 1787, m. Richard Holly.
288 John C., b. Oct. 15, 1788, m. Almìra Jackson, Apr. 28, 1841.
289 Samuel D., b. Oct. 15, 1788, unm.
290 Aaron, b. Aug. 13, 1793, m. Sarah Writer, Aug. 2, 1817, 8 children, m. 2d, Elizabeth Brown, Apr. 1, 1824, 6 children; m. 3d, Helen O. Horton, Dec. 31, 1839, 2 children.
291 Nancy, b. Aug. 13, 1793.

138 AARON AND HEYLTE (VAN GARDEN) KORTRIGHT, issue:

292 Dorothy, bap. Sept. 18, 1785, m. Peter Hooghtaling, Dec. 17, 1803.
293 Jacobus, bap. Apr. 22, 1787.
294 Petrus, bap. Mar. 29, 1789.

139 JOHN AND JANNETJE (MIDDAGH) KORTRIGHT, issue:

295 Margriet, bap. Oct. 17, 1773, m. James Windfield, Feb. 4, 1808.
296 Arie, bap. June 14, 1775, m. Elizabeth Onstott, Oct. 13, 1805.
297 Nicholas, bap. Aug. 16, 1782.

142 HENDRICK W. AND CATRINÀ (MIDDAGH) KORTRIGHT, issue:

298 Mary De Witt, bap. Jan. 28, 1759, m. Aaron Westbrook.
+299 William, bap. May 1, 1763, m. Elizabeth Brink.
300 Janitje, bap. Dec. 1, 1765.
+301 Hendrick J., bap. Dec. 2, 1771, m. Catrina Van Garden, Sept. 1, 1796.
302 Cathrina, bap. Nov. 1, 1780, m. Martin Davenport, Dec. 30, 1806.

143 ELIÀS AND DEBORAH (COMSTOCK) KORTRIGHT, issue:

303 Anna, bap. June 12, 1768, m. Moses Brink, Mar. 11, 1787.
304 Margriet, bap. Sept. 22, 1771, m. Charles Dutcher, May 19, 1791.
305 Febe, bap. Oct. 17, 1773, m. Stephen Monroe, Dec. 21, 1789.
306 Josias, bap. June 14, 1775.
307 Elias, bap. July 9, 1777.
308 William, bap. May 1, 1785.

145 JOSIAS W. AND CORNELIA (COOL) KORTRIGHT, issue:

+309 William J., bap. Apr. 25, 1771, m. Christina Myers.
310 Blandina, bap. Nov. 25, 1776, m. Abraham Courtright, Oct. 10, 1801.
311 Elizabeth, bap. Aug. 1784.
312 Gideon, bap. Mar. 5, 1786.
313 Andriss, bap. Nov. 29, 1789.

149 JOHANNES AND SUSANNA (KITTEL) KORTRIGHT, issue:

314 Gisbert, bap. Apr. 3, 1763.
315 Samuel, bap. Feb. 9, 1767, m. (?) Anny Kyte, Nov. 16, 1794.
316 Susanna, bap. Aug. 24, 1777, m. William Hooghtaling.
317 Johannes, bap. Nov. 1, 1780.
318 Elizabeth, b. 1772, m. (?) Joseph Westbrook, Aug. 13, 1797.

153 Samuel and Margriet (Westfael) Kortright, issue:
319 Elizabeth, bap. Nov. 25, 1776, m. John Williams, Apr. 28, 1796.
320 Lydia, bap. Nov. 1, 1780, m. William Bennett, May 3, 1804.
321 Reuben, bap. July 25, 1790, m. Deborah Bedell, Oct. 9, 1808; m. 2d, Elizabeth Van Etten, Apr. 1830.
322 Petrus, bap. June 28, 1798.

155 Salomon and Cornelia (Cool) Kortright, issue:
323 Catryntie, bap. Feb. 13, 1758, m. Gerrett Brink, Nov. 8, 1776.
324 Hendrick, bap. Nov. 22, 1759.

158 Daniel and Antje (Westbrook) Kortright, issue:
325 Gedion, bap. Nov. 30, 1770.
326 Solomon, bap. Apr. 20, 1784.
327 Janneke, bap. Sept. 6, 1781.

159 Moses and Antje (Van Etten) Kortright, issue:
328 Annatje, bap. Nov. 25, 1770.
329 Levi, bap. Aug. 27, 1772, m.
330 Safferyn, bap. Oct. 29, 1780.
331 Maria, bap. June 22, 1783, m. Abraham Decker, 1809.

167 Jonas and Elizabeth (Davis) Kortright, issue:
332 Jacob, bap. Feb. 9, 1773.
+333 Petrus, bap. Nov. 25, 1776, m. Catharine Cebler (or Hebler).

169 Jacob and Femmetje (Deenmark) Kortright, issue:
334 Elizabeth, bap. Feb. 9, 1773, m. Adrian Line.
335 Jacob, bap. June 14, 1775.
336 Antie, bap. Aug. 31, 1781, m. (?) Isaac Swartwout.

171 Solomon and Anna (Ayers) Kortright, issue:
337 Sarah, bap. Aug. 31, 1781, m. Andrew Van Sickle, Sept. 8, 1800.
338 Phoebe Ayers, m. Elnathan Stevens.

Sylvester and Annatje (Davis) Kortright, issue:
339 Jauneke, bap. Oct. 29, 1780.
340 Wilhelmus, bap. Aug. 18, 1782.
341 Deborah, bap. Apr. 20, 1784.

175 Simon and Catharina (Ennes) Kortright, issue:
342 Maria, bap. May 5, 1785, m. Jacob Kyte, Jan. 22, 1804.

179 Cornelis and Tjaetje (Kortright) Cortright, issue:
343 Hendrick, bap. Aug. 21, 1748.

179 Cornelis and Helena (Roosekrans) Cortright, issue:
344 Abraham, bap. Dec. 9, 1750.

181 DANIEL AND RUSSIE (VAN AKEN) CORTRIGHT, issue:

- 345   Hester, bap. Oct. 14, 1753, m. Jeremiah Vandermark, Oct. 29, 1771.
- 346   Jannetje, bap. Feb. 2, 1755, m. Samuel Decker.
- 347   Moses, bap. June 17, 1757.
- 348   Levi, bap. 1759, m. Sarah Decker, Mar. 31, 1790.
- 349   Gideon, bap. Mar. 20, 1761, m. Rachel Decker, Nov. 24, 1785.
- 350   David, bap. Feb. 6, 1763, m. Elizabeth Davenport.
- 351   Joseph, bap. July 4, 1765, m. Elizabeth Sly, Nov. 3, 1788.
- +352   Daniel, bap. Aug. 30, 1772, m. Elizabeth Swartwout.
- 353   Cornelius, m. Hannah Decker, July 6, 1797.
- 354   Caty, m. John Decker, Feb. 8, 1787.

182 BENJAMIN AND CATRINA (HOVER) CORTRIGHT, issue:

- +355   Cornelus, bap. Apr. 15, 1764, m. Catharine Kennedy, Oct. 1, 1786.
- 356   Anna, bap. July 27, 1766, m. Nathan Draper.
- 357   Sarah, m. Chareck Rosecrans, Mar. 2, 1788.
- 358   Hendrick, bap. Sept. 26, 1771, m. Rachel Gore, about 1798.
- 359   Johannes, bap. May 22, 1774, m. Mary Abbott, Dec. 10, 1800.
- 360   Catrina, bap. Aug. 25, 1781, (b. 1778), probably m. Manuel Decker.

184 WILLIAM ENNES AND SARAH (HANDSHAW) CORTRIGHT, issue:

- +361   William, bap. Aug. 8, 1768, m. Cattrina Helm, Aug. 2, 1787.
- +362   Johannes, bap. May 22, 1774, m. Mary Clark, Sept. 14, 1797.
- 363   Mary, m. Benjamin Vandermark.

185 ABRAHAM AND NEELTIE (SWARTWOUT) CORTRIGHT, issue:

- +364   Anthony, bap. Dec. 3, 1771, m. Lena Emmons.
- 365   Jentie E., bap. Mar. 4, 1772, m. John Vandermark, Dec. 25, 1792.
- 366   Lena, bap. June 15, 1775.
- 367   Cornelia, bap. June 8, 1777, m. Abraham Westfall, Sept. 16, 1810.

187 JACOBUS (OR JAMES) AND ANNA (QUICK) CORTRIGHT, issue:

- 368   Sarah, bap. Sept. 19, 1771, m. Jacob Myers, Mar. 5, 1789.
- 369   Thomas, bap. May 22, 1774.
- 370   Annie, bap. June 15, 1775, m. (?) Isaac Swartwout.

187 JACOBUS (OR JAMES) AND JANNETIE (VAN AKEN) CORTRIGHT, issue:

- 371   Elizabeth C., bap. Sept. 10, 1785, at Smithfield.
- 372   Levi, bap. Sept. 10, 1785, at Smithfield.
- 373   James, bap. May 13, 1787, at Smithfield.
- 374   Mary, bap. June 8, 1790, at Smithfield.

189 JOHN, JR., AND MARIA (VAN VLIET) CORTRIGHT, issue:

375   Samuel, bap. Apr. 2, 1763, m. (?) Anny Kyte, Nov. 16, 1794.
376   Derick, bap. June 25, 1764.
377   John, bap. Sept. 28, 1766.
378   Rachel, bap. May 22, 1774, m. Benjamin Decker.

190 CHRISTOPHER AND MARTHA (MILLER) CORTRIGHT, issue:

379   Christina E., bap. Sept. 19, 1771.
380   Thomas, bap. June 15, 1775.
381   Elizabeth, bap. June 8, 1777, m. (?) Joseph Westbrook, Aug. 13, 1797.

192 ELISHA AND ALIDA (DINGMAN) CORTRIGHT, issue:

382   Cornelia, bap. Nov. 20, 1768, m. Emanuel Hoover.
383   Eva, bap. May 22, 1774, m. Aaron Writer.

193 ABRAHAM VAN KAMPEN AND EFFIE (DRAKE) CORTRIGHT, issue ·

384   John, b. Feb. 26, 1779, m. Elizabeth Grubb.

196 LAWRENCE AND MARIA (KORTRIGHT) KORTRIGHT, issue:

385   Jacobus, bap. Aug. 12, 1780, m. Cornelia Decker.
386   Mattheus, bap. May 2, 1791.

200 CORNELIUS AND JEMIMA (MORRIS) KORTRIGHT, issue:

387   Harriet, 388 Elizabeth, 389 Benjamin, 390 Maria, 391 Jane, 392 Morris, 393 Cornelius.

205 HENRICUS AND MARIA (OOSTERHOUT) KORTRIGHT, issue:

394   Abraam, bap. July 3, 1796.
395   Lawrence, bap. Mar. 8, 1798.
396   Jannetje, bap. Jan. 1, 1800.
397   Moses, bap. Apr. 14, 1802, m. Catharine Depuy.
398   Elizabeth, bap. Aug. 12, 1804.
399   Levi, bap. Oct. 19, 1806.
400   John, bap. July 8, 1809.
401   Cornelius, bap. Aug. 22, 1812.

210 HENDRICK AND CORNELIA (DECKER) CORTRIGHT, issue:

402   Abraham D., bap. June 15, 1775.
403   Cornelius, bap. June 8, 1777.
404   Isaac, bap. July 2, 1780.
405   Elizabeth, bap. Apr. 24, 1784.

214 ISAAC AND SUSANNA (DAILEY) CORTRIGHT, issue:

406   Margaret, bap. May 24, 1795.
407   Leah, b. June 18, 1800.
408   Abraham Peter, b. Sept. 21, 1801.

SEVENTH GENERATION.

282 CAPT. JOHN AND CATHARINE (SEAMAN) KORTRIGHT, issue:

409 John L.
410 Edmund.
411 Robert.
412 Nicholas G., m. Sarah Allaire.
413 Eliza, m. Nicholas Cruger.
414 Hester Mary, m. Billop B. Seaman.

Capt. John Kortright (282), married May 2, 1793, Catharine, daughter of Edmund Seaman, who, after his death in 1810, married Henry B. Livingston.

His farm on Harlem Lane, with the new mansion built west of the Lane, descended to his children, as above.

299 WILLIAM AND ELIZABETH (BRINK) CORTRIGHT, issue:

415 Hester, bap. June 22, 1788, m. Peter Q. Howell.
416 Catrina, bap. June 5, 1791, m. William Van Garden, July 3, 1813.

301 HENDRICK JANSEN AND CATRINA (VAN GARDEN) CORTRIGHT, issue:

417 William, bap. Sept. 7, 1797, m. Jemima Huff, 1819.
418 Susanna, bap. Mar. 25, 1799.

309 WILLIAM J. AND CHRISTINA (MYERS) CORTRIGHT, issue:

419 Hannah, bap. Aug. 24, 1800.
420 Maria, bap. Mar. 29, 1801.
421 Susanna, bap. Aug. 12, 1803.
422 John Drake, bap. Mar. 22, 1815.
423 Sally, bap. Mar. 22, 1815.

333 PETER AND CATHARINE (CEBLER) CORTRIGHT, issue:

424 Jacob E., b. Aug. 16, 1802.
425 Samuel, b. Sept. 20, 1807.
426 Hannah, b. 1809.
427 Jane Y., b. Feb. 19, 1813.

352 DANIEL AND ELIZABETH (SWARTWOUT) CORTRIGHT, issue:

428 Mary, bap. Aug. 3, 1794.
429 Thomas, bap. Oct. 3, 1803.
430 William, bap. June 16, 1811.

355 CORNELIUS AND CATHARINE (KENNEDY) CORTRIGHT, issue:

431 Mary, bap. Jan. 27, 1788.
432 Benjamin, bap. July 3, 1789.
433 Caty, bap. Nov. 1, 1790.
434 John, bap. Nov. 1, 1790.

361 William and Cattrina (Helm) Cortright, issue:
435 Samuel, bap. Feb. 8, 1789.
436 Hester, bap. June 5, 1791.
437 Joannes, bap. Sept. 14, 1794.

362 John and Mary (Clark) Cortright, issue:
438 Sarah, b. Aug. 18, 1798.

364 Anthony and Lena (Emmons) Cortright, issue:
439 Abram, bap. May 27, 1792.

————

The following Cortrights are unidentified as to parentage but appear in the church records, viz:—

Petrus, who m. Maria Westfael, about 1754.
Daniel, m. Plony Westfael and had issue:
    July, bap. Aug. 16, 1795.
    Jannetje, bap. Sept. 3, 1797.
    Samuel, bap. Sept. 10, 1800.
    Simon, bap. Aug. 8, 1807.
    William, bap. Feb. 12, 1808.
Cornelius, m. Hannah Steele and had issue:
    Sarah, bap. Feb. 4, 1816.
    Nelly, bap. Jan. 31, 1819.
    Mariah, bap. Oct. 1, 1820.
    Amanda, bap. July 13, 1823.
    Daniel, bap. Oct. 2, 1825.
Marya Kortright, m. Evert Roos Westbrook, Apr. 24, 1752.
Richard Cortwright, witness to will, Albany, Dec. 15, 1753.
Hendrik Kortregt, who m. Cornelia Hendrickse, and had Joseph, bap.
    Sept. 22, 1745, at the Dutch church, Hackensack, N. J.
Michael Kortright, who m. Mary Huson, June 23, 1765.
Michael McKeel, an early settler of Yorktown, who had Uriah, John,
    and Isaac. Isaac had Jesse, Jacob, Caleb, Joshua, Isaac and George.
Peter Cortrite, b. 1768, d. at Geneva, Dec. 13, 1861.

THE COURTRIGHT FAMILY OF THE WYOMING VALLEY, PA.

FIRST GENERATION.

1. JAN BASTIAENSEN, son of Bastiaen Van Kortryk, came, as we have seen, from the small town of Beest, in Gelderland, Holland, sailing April 16, 1663, in the ship Spotted Cow, accompanied by his brother Michiel, and their respective families. Jan was the owner of a bouwery, or farm, on Staten Island, spent part of his time at Harlem, but there is very little recorded of his early history.

His children, all born at Beest, came with him, and finally settled at Harlem, a small village eight miles north of New Amsterdam, their names being Cornelis, Hendrick, Laurens and Belitie.

SECOND GENERATION

2. HENDRICK JANSEN, (VAN CORTRIGHT), soon after his arrival, purchased land near Stuyvesant's Bouwery, on Feb. 12th, 1669, but did not long hold it, and with his brother Laurens, went to Esopus, (Kingston) Ulster County, New York, where he married on Dec. 14, 1672, Catharine, dau. of Hans and Elsje (Pieters, van Hamburg) Webber. The court record of this marriage states she was "born in New York"; Hans Webber was appointed Captain at arms to the garrison at Fort Amsterdam, on Sept. 28, 1647, and died in 1649, and his widow married in 1650, Matthys Capito, removed to Esopus, where she was killed by the Indians in 1663. Hendrick evidently lived at Harlem for a time, as his first child was born there, in 1674, but he afterward purchased land at Mombaccus, Township of Rochester, where he raised his family.

Hendrick Jansen Cortrecht was among the list of early freeholders and inhabitants of the town of Rochester, who on January 20th, 1714, was assessed the sum of six shillings, ten pence, he at that time being estimated to be worth fifty-five pounds sterling in assessable wealth. On Sept. 22, 1703, his name appears on the "Quit rent" list.

He died in 1741, aged 93 years, and his wife in 1740, having had children, Jan, Hendrick, Cornelis, Geertie, Arie, Antie, Jacob, Louwerens, Jannetje, Pieter, and Catryn.

THIRD GENERATION

3. CORNELIS HENDRICKSEN CORTRIGHT, third child of Hendrick, was baptized in the Reformed Dutch Church at New York, the record being, "Cornelis, son of Hendrick Janszen and Catharyn Hans, baptized Nov. 3d, 1680, the sponsors being Jacob Janszen (Decker), Belitie Jans, and Reyer Michielszen." His marriage is thus recorded in the Dutch Church, at Kingston, "Cornelis Hendricksen, j. m., born in Mombackes, and Christina Roosekrans, j.d., born in Kingstouwn, and both residing in Mombackes, married December 26, 1701."

For several years he lived at Rochester, where with his brothers, he was a prominent man, but later in life removed to Marbletown, not far from Rochester, where several of his children were born, and after living there several years, he probably removed to the Minisink district, in Monroe County, Penn., as his wife joined the church there, known as the Smithfield church, June 23, 1745, "upon the representation of satisfactory certificates, in the presence of Niclas Du Pay, elder of the church." He and his wife witnessed the baptism of a grand-child in 1736, so probably he was living in Monroe Co., Pa., at the time, which then was included in Northampton County.

His name was written in the church records variously as, Cortregt, Cortrecht, Cortreght, etc., and sometimes with a K.

The records of the church at Kingston show his children were, Hendrick, Magdalena, Catrina, Johannes, Sara, Cornelis, and Benjamin, all of whom came to the Minisink district, except the latter two, who remained in Ulster County.

Harmen Hendricksen Roosekrans (or Rosenkrans) came from Bergen, Norway, about 1655, he then being forty-three years of age.

He had been admitted a "small" burgher of New York in 1658, and on March 3, 1657, m. Magdaleen (Madeleen) Dircks, a dau. of Dirck and Christina (Vinge) Volckertsen, and widow of Cornelis Hendricksen van Dort, "Caper," or privateersman, who was killed by the Indians in 1655. Before Feb. 7, 1662, Harmen and his wife removed to Esopus, afterward known as Wiltwick, (and under the English,—Kingston), Ulster County, New York, where he engaged in farming.

Prior to his removal there, he had been a soldier at Kingston, and was the only captive to escape from the Indians after their uprising Sept. 29th, 1659, in reprisal of the Dutch attack, he having been captured, bound and exposed to the rays of the autumn sun. (N. Y. Col. Mss.)

He and his wife sold liquor to the Indians, and for this and other matters, were frequently in Court, and in 1684, as one of the petitioners at Kingston seeking leave to elect town officers, etc., he was fined by Governor Dongan. Harmen and his wife acquired considerable land in Ulster County, where they lived for many years, raising a large family of children, who were, so far as known:

Alexander, bap. N. Y., Apr. 12, 1661, m. Marritjen De Pue.
Annatje, bap. N. Y., Aug. 27, 1662, d. young.
Rachel, bap. N. Y., Aug. 21, 1663, m. Gysbert Van Garden.
Harmanus, bap. May 2, 1666, no record.
Anna, m. Humphrey Davenport, Apr. 18, 1684.
Hendrick, m. Annatje Vredenburg, Oct. 26, 1721, m. 2d, Antje Delva, and m. 3d, Gerretje Van Benschoten.
Christina, m. Cornelis Hendricksen Cortright, Dec. 26, 1701.
Dirck, m. Wyntie Kierstede, wid. of Jan De Witt.
Sarah, unm., made will, June 17, 1726, naming her mother, Magdalena, and Hendrick, Derick, Alexander, Rachel and Christian, and Hendrick, son of Christian.

Dirck Volkertsen, (Noorman), was an early settler and prominent farmer in Brooklyn, at Bushwick Creek, where he built his home in 1640, and in 1649, he and his wife, Christina Vinge, became members of the Reformed Dutch Church at New Amsterdam; they had several children, among these being, Magdaleen, who m. Harmen Hendricksen Roosekrans, in 1657.

Gulian, (or Julian) Vinge, and his wife, Adrianna Cuveille, came from Valenciennes, France, in 1613 or 1614, probably on a trading expedition, as traders came soon after Hendrick Hudson discovered the river now bearing his name, but at this time there was no settlement, the first one being established in 1623.

He had children, b. in France, Rachel, m. Cornelis Van Tienhoven; Maria, m. Abraham Verplanck; Christina, m. Dirck Volckertsen; and John, b. in New Amsterdam, *circa* 1614, who m. Emmerens Van Nieuwerzluys, m. 2d, Weiske Huytes, widow of Andries Andriessen.

John was the first child of European parents b. in New Amsterdam, and probably in all the territory north of Virginia, eleven years before Sarah Rapalje, and at the earliest period compatible with the sojourn of any Hollanders upon our territory, so there must have been at least *one* European woman in the country at that early period.

FOURTH GENERATION

4. HENDRICK CORNELISSEN CORTRIGHT, b. in Rochester township, Ulster County, N. Y., was bap. in the Dutch Reformed Church at Kingston, which is thus recorded, "baptized March 29, 1703, Hendrick, son of

Cornelis Hendricksen and Christina Roosekrans; witnesses and sponsors Hannes Roosekrans, Magdalena Roosekrans."

His marriage is also recorded there, "Hendrik Kortregt, j.m., b. in Raysester (Rochester), and Jannetjen Ennes, j.d., b. in Mormeltown (Marbletown), and both residing in Mormeltown. Banns registered 11 Sept., m. Nov. 6, 1724," by Dominie Petrus Vas.

He resided in Marbletown till about 1736, but came to the Minisink prior to 1739, and in 1745, bought from William Ennes a farm in Delaware Township, Bucks County, (afterward Northampton County, and now Pike) in Pennsylvania, located between Egypt Mills and Bushkill, .where he lived the remainder of his life.

Prior to his purchase of this farm, he lived at Walpeck, Sussex County, New Jersey, in what was known as the "lower neighborhood," being listed as a tax-payer, with Hendrick Hendricksen, Abraham, Ary, William and Hendrick Cortregt, and Jan Van Vliet, Samuel Swartwout and others, and was one of the pioneer settlers there.

In 1772 and 1781, he was assessed taxes in Delaware Township, Northampton County, (now Pike) and for his day, was a successful farmer, and highly respected man.

Both he and his wife were members of the Reformed Dutch Church known as the "Walpeck Congregation," situated across the Delaware River at Walpeck, Sussex County, N. J., where several of his later children were baptized. He d. in 1787, leaving a will, dated March 27, 1787, proved April 20, 1787, which will interest his descendants, as it proves the descent of many, being also a quaint document, and is as follows:—

"In the Name of God Amen I Henry Cor. Courtright of Dillaware Township County of Northampton and State of Pennsylvania yeoman; being through the abundant Mercy and Goodness of God tho weak in body yet of a sound and perfect understanding and memory Do Constitute this my last Will and Testament and desire it may be recd. by all as such. Imprimis I most humbly Bequith my soul to God my maker Be seeching him most Gracious Acceptance of it through the all Sufficient merrits and Mediation of my Most Compassionate Redeemer Jesus Christ my Saviour Amen Blessed be God.

Imprimis I give my Body to the Earth from whence it was taken in full assurance of its Reasurection from thence at the last day, as for my Burial I desire it may be decent at the discretion of my Executors herein after named. As to my Wordly Estate I will and positively Order that first of all my Honist Debts be first paid Item I give and Bequeath unto my grandson Henry Courtright son of my eldest son Cornelis Courtright deceased the sum of thirty two pounds of Good and Lawful Money of Pennsylvania to be paid one year after my death Item I give and Bequeath unto my son Daniel Courtright the sum of One Pound of like money as aforesaid Itim I give unto my Well beloved grandson Cornelius Courtright son of my son Daniel Courtright the sum of thirty Pounds Lawful money of Pennsylvania to paid to him when he arrives at the age of Twenty one Years by my Executors. Itim I give Devise and Bequith unto my Grandson John Courtright son of my son Benj. Courtright deceased the like sum of thirty Pounds Currant Lawful Money of the place aforesaid to be paid unto him when he arrives at the adge of twenty one years Itim I give and Bequeath unto my Grandson William Courtright son of my son Will. Ennis Courtright the sum of Thirty pounds of like money as aforesaid and to be paid to him when he arrives at the adge of Twenty one years Itim I give and Bequeith unto my Grandson Anthony son of my son Abraham Courtright deceased the like sum of thirty pound Currant Money of Pennsylvania to be paid to him at the adge of Twenty one years Itim I give and Bequeith to my grandson Daniel Vandermark son of my daughter Jeane Courtright Vandermark the sum of thirty pounds of like money as aforesaid to be paid to him when he arrives at the adge of Twenty one years Itim I give and devise unto my grandson Jonathan Hover son of my daughter Cornela Courtright Hover thirty pounds Currant Money of Pennsylvania to be paid unto him when he arrives at the adge of Twenty one years Itim I give unto my poor son William Ennes Courtright the sum of Thirty pound of like money as aforesaid to be paid unto him or his Hears at the discretion of my Executors Item I give and Bequith unto my son Jeames Courtright the sum of thirty pounds Currant money of Pennsylvania to be paid to him one Year after my decease Itim I give and Bequith unto my grandaughter Sarah Courtright Daughter of my son Benj. Courtright, deceased, tinn pounds of like money as above to be paid at the discretion of my Executors Itim I give and Bequith unto my Grand Daughter Jeane Hover, Daughter of my Daughter Cornela Hover my Bed and all my Beding. Imprimis I will make ordain Constitute and appoint my trusty friend Manuel Hover and my well beloved grandson Cornelis Cortright son of my son Benj Courtright deceased my sole Executors of this my last Will and Testament and do order them my said Executors to pay all and every of the above sums and legasye as they come due according to the entent and meaning of this my Last Will and desire and if any of my above Grandsons shuld die before they artive to adge then their shares shall desend on the next youndest in that Family. Itim I give devise and Bequith all my remaining Estate Rail and Personable unto my Executors hereinbefore mentioned for their kind services and other Good causes me thereunto Movin. And I do hereby revoke disanull and make void all my former and other Wills and Testaments heretofore made and don Ritifieng and confirming this to be my Last Will and desire In Witness whereof I have hereunto set my hand and fixed my seal this twenty seventh day of March one thousand seven Hundred and eighty seven.

Henry Cortright (Seal)

Sined sealed published and declared by the said Testator as and for his Last Will and Testament in the presents of us, who in his presents and at his request have hereunto subscribed our names as Witnesses.

Ezekiel Schoonover   Moses Cole   Thomas Landon

From this will it is seen that Hendrick was a man of religious convictions, and for the times in which he lived, left a considerable estate.

William Innes (or as written by the Dutch, Ennes) was a son of Rev. Alexander Innes, of Scotch descent, Chaplain of New York in 1686, and "Presbiter of the Church of England" in 1692. He married Cornelia Viervant, in Kingston, 1686, who was the only child of Cornelis Arents Viervant, and his wife, Jeanne Le Sueur, whom he married at Kingston, in 1668. Cornelis Arents Viervant was a native of Lexmont, in the Land of Vianen, Utrecht, who first lived at Kingston, but died at Fordham, 1675.

His wife, Jeanne, was the sister of Francois Le Sueur, the ancestor of those who bear his name, both born at Challe-Mesnil or Colmenil, a small market town three miles south of Dieppe, in Normandy, who sailed for New Amsterdam in 1657, neither being married. They first lived at Flatbush, were pioneers at Harlem in 1660, which they left in 1663, removing to Esopus (Kingston). William and Cornelia (Viervant) Ennes had Jannetje, bap. at Kingston, July 17; 1703, m. Hendrick Cortright, Nov. 6, 1724:

Hendrick Cornelissen and Jannetje (Ennes) Cortright, issue:—
Cornelis, bap. June 27, 1725, m. Tjaetje Kortright, Dec. 6, 1747 m. 2d, Helena Roosekrans, Apr. 8, 1750.
Catrina, bap. Feb. 12, 1727, probably d. young.
Daniel, bap. Apr. 13, 1729, m. Russie Van Aken, Mar. 1, 1752.
Benjamin, b. 1731, m. Catrina Hover, about 1762.
Johannes, bap. May 19, 1736, unm.
William E., bap. Oct. 31, 1739, m. Sarah Handshaw, Aug. 8, 1768.
Abraham, bap. July 23, 1741, m. Neeltie Swartwout, before 1771.

Jenneke, bap. Jan. 13, 1745, m. Johannes Vandermark, before 1763.

James, bap. Mar. 8, 1747, m. Anna Quick, m. 2d, Jannetie Van Aken.

Cornelia, bap. June 21, 1749, m. Henry Hover, before 1766.

Of these children, Cornelis d. in 1752, Daniel in 1788, Johannes in 1772, Benjamin and Abraham before 1787. In his will, dated Feb. 8, 1772, Johannes gives his brothers William, Abraham and Benjamin a bequest of forty pounds each, and mentions no wife or children.

James, Daniel, Benjamin, William and Abraham served as soldiers in the Revolution, William being severely wounded and crippled for life, and thus referred to by his father as "his poor son," in his will.

FIFTH GENERATION

5. BENJAMIN CORTRIGHT, born at Marbletown, Ulster County, New York 1731, was probably baptized the same year at the Kingston Church, but there is no record of this, as the first leaves of Vol. III, of the Church records, covering the period from April 12, 1730, to January 1732, are missing. He probably came with his parents to the Minisink district in 1736, and his name first appears on the records of the "Walpeck Congregation" as a sponsor in 1750 and again in 1753.

On January 12th, 1756, he and his brother John enlisted as soldiers from the Province of Pennsylvania, in the French and Indian war, under the command of Captain John Van Etten.

In 1772 and again in 1781, he was assessed for taxes in Delaware Township, Northampton County, Penn., where he probably owned property, but he may have remained on his father's farm during his life.

During the Revolution, he served as a soldier, Class 3, of the 6th Battalion, Northampton County Militia, his name appearing on the muster roll for May 14, 1778, under the command of Col. Jacob Stroud and Captain John Van Etten.

His name also appears as an enlisted soldier, of the 3d Class of the 1st Company, 6th Battalion, in 1780; the 4th Company, 5th Battalion in 1781; and again in the same Company in 1782, his name being written on the muster rolls variously as Cartright, Cortrigt, Curtright and Courtright.

In his will of March 27th, 1787, Benjamin's father refers to him as deceased, so he probably died between 1782 and 1787.

The name of his wife was Catrina Hover, (or as now written, Catharine Hoover) whom he married about 1762. She was probably a sister of Henry, who m. Cornelia Cortright, and of Capt. Emanuel

Hover, the Hover's owning an adjoining farm, and she may have been a daughter of Johannes Michael Huber, who came in 1731, and m. Catharine Rose in 1742.

The name Huber is derived from an old word, "hutre," meaning the possessor of a small tract of land, or farm, which indicates this family is descended from a clan of Swiss farmers, as the Canton of Zurich, Switzerland, was the original home of the Hubers, many of them still residing there, with records dating back over 800 years.

During the civil and religious disturbances of the 17th century, many of the Hubers were driven from their mountain homes, and fled to Germany, France and other European countries, ultimately coming to America. The ship records at Philadelphia show that nearly fifty Hubers, not including women or children, landed there prior to the Revolution.

In the course of time the spelling of the name has changed, so now the variations are Hover, Hoover, Huver, Hoober and Hooper.

BENJAMIN AND CATHARINE (HOVER) CORTRIGHT, issue:

+6 Cornelus, b. Mar. 7, 1764, bap. Apr. 15, 1764, at Walpeck, m. Catharine Kennedy, Oct. 1, 1786.
Hannah, b. 1766, bap. July 27, 1766, at Walpeck, m. Nathan Draper, about 1786.
Sarah, b. 1768, m. Chareck Rosecrans, Mar. 2, 1788.
+7 Hendrick, b. May 10, 1771, bap. Sept. 26, 1771, at Walpeck, m. Rachel Gore, about 1798.
+8 Johannes, b. April 4, 1774, bap. May 22, 1774, at Walpeck, m. Mary Abbott, Dec. 10, 1800.
Catharine, b. June 1778, bap. Aug. 25, 1781, at Walpeck, probably m. Manuel Decker, before 1809.

SIXTH GENERATION

+6. CORNELIUS CORTRIGHT, (who thus wrote his name, and as it appears on his monument), was born March 7th, 1764, on the farm of his grandfather, located in Lehman Township, Pike County, Pennsylvania, (but then in Delaware Township, Northampton County) this farm being situated on the bank of the Delaware River, near Port Jervis, and not far from the Delaware Water Gap.

He was baptized April 15, 1764, in the Reformed Dutch Church known as the "Walpeck Congregation," the record being, "Cornelus, son of Benjamin Cortregt and Catrina Hover; witnesses and sponsors, Henderick Hover and Cornelia Hover," Domine Thomas Romaine officiating.

He was one of the executors of his grand-father's will in 1787;

HOME OF HON. CORNELIUS CORTRIGHT (6), PLAINS, LUZERNE COUNTY, PA.

during the Revolution, he enlisted as a soldier of the 4th Company, 5th Battalion, Northampton County Militia, June, 1782, his name being written on the muster roll as Cornelus Courtryt. His name was also on the muster roll of Captain John Van Etten's Company of the 5th Battalion, Northampton County Militia, July 31, 1784, on the expedition to Wyoming, this being probably his first appearance in the Wyoming Valley.

On Oct. 1st, 1786, he married Catharine, daughter of John and Maria (Van Vliet) Kennedy, at Plains, Luzerne Co., Pa., (see Kennedy family).

In November, 1787, he was elected Ensign of the Militia Company from the Upper District of Wilkes Barre, (Daniel Gore, Captain), in the Battalion commanded by Col. Mathias Hollenback.

He made his first purchase of land from William Hooker Smith, on Dec. 30th, 1789, and his second from Timothy Pickering, Sept. 19th, 1791, settled in Plains township, acquired additional land, and lived there during his life, where he was a highly respected man, holding numerous public offices.

He was commissioned Justice of the Peace Jan. 1st, 1806, continuing as such until 1840; was one of the Commissioners for Luzerne County in 1813, 1814, 1815, 1830 and 1832; was a member of the Pennsylvania State Legislature in 1820, 1821 and 1823, and a candidate for State Senator in 1816, being defeated for the latter office.

"For a long series of years, he was one of the most active, public spirited and prominent men of the county."

He died May 25th, 1848, and his wife, May 12th, 1846, having had eleven children, who inherited his estate.

+7. HENRY CORTRIGHT, brother of Cornelius, was born on the ancestral farm in Pike County, May 10, 1771, baptized at Walpeck, Sept. 26, 1771, died Mar. 27, 1864, the son of Benjamin Cortregt and Catrina Hover, as the church record shows, and came to the Wyoming Valley soon after his brother Cornelius did, where he also purchased a farm, settling at Plains.

Several years later he sold his farm at Plains, many years before the value of the underlying coal was realized, and removed to Exeter, where he lived for fifteen years, having bought another farm there, but finally removed to Franklin (now Orange), where he bought a large tract of land, of one hundred sixty-six acres, where he continued to reside until his death, March 27, 1864.

As shown by the report of Jesse Fell, Brigade Inspector, he was elected Lieutenant of the 2d Regiment, 1st Battalion, Light Infantry Company, of the Militia of Luzerne County, Feb. 3d, 1794.

"He was a man of force in the community, of sterling qualities, did not aspire to office, yet bore his share of responsibilities, commanding the respect and esteem of all who knew him."

He married Rachel, daughter of Capt. Daniel and Mary (Park) Gore, about 1798, who died April 11, 1848. (see Gore family).

+8. John Cortright, brother of Cornelius and Henry, was born Apr. 4, 1774, on the farm in Pike (then Northampton) County, baptized at Walpeck May 22, 1774, the church record being "Johannes, son of Benjamin Kortregt and Catrina Hover, by Dr. Jacob R. Hardenberg."

When a young man he inherited a sum of money from the estate of his grandfather, and as did his brothers, came to the Wyoming Valley about the same time, where he became an extensive land owner, settling also in Plains township, where he resided on his farm until his death, Dec. 1, 1822.

For several years, after his sons attained manhood, he kept the tavern at Plains, and was also the first post-master there.

In his will, dated August 29th, 1822, and proved March 23d, 1823, he signs his name "John Cortright," and having made suitable provision for his wife and other children, he devised his landed estate equally to his sons, Cornelius and John Draper Courtright, and directs that his coal bed, in Wilkes Barre Township, near the Pittston line, be disposed of for the benefit of these sons, or the right thereof be vested in them. This coal bed was a tract of about thirty-one acres.

Catharine Cortright and John Cortright, son of Catharine, of Jacobs Plains, widow, conveyed land by deed dated Dec. 20, 1791, the witnesses being Cornelius Cortright and Charrick D. Rosenkrans; and on April 16, 1800, John Cortright conveyed land to Catharine Cortright, mother of said John, witnessed by Cornelus and Henry Cortright, so it is evident that Catharine Hover, the mother of Cornelius, Henry and John Cortright, resided in Plains at the dates mentioned.

John Cortright married Mary (called Polly), daughter of John and Alice (Fuller) Abbott, Dec. 10th, 1800. (see Abbott family).

SEVENTH GENERATION

6 Hon. Cornelius and Catharine (Kennedy) Cortright, issue:

+9 Mary, b. July 29, 1787, d. Oct. 27, 1836, m. John Murphy, Jan. 13, 1817.

+10 Benjamin, b. Mar. 19, 1789, d. Jan. 22, 1867, m. Clarissa Williams, Jan. 23, 1820.

HOME OF JOHN CORTRIGHT, PLAINS, LUZERNE COUNTY, PA.

+11 Catharine, b. Oct. 11, 1790, m. Isaiah Tyson, Jan. 5, 1811.
+12 John, b. Oct. 12, 1790, d. May 16, 1830, m. Lois Searle, Jan. 7, 1816.
+13 Henry, b. Sept. 4, 1792, m. Sarah Bidleman.
 14 Elizabeth, b. Mar. 14, 1795, d. Mar. 2, 1804.
+15 Hannah, b. Feb. 7, 1798, d. May 3, 1892, m. John Abbott, Mar. 11, 1830.
 16 Lucinda, b. Feb. 2, 1801, d. Apr. 5, 1823.
+17 Eleanor, b. Sept. 13, 1804, d. Mar. 10, 1886, m. William Abbott, Nov. 2, 1824.
+18 Elizabeth, b. June 25, 1807, d. 1890, m. Charles M. Wright, Jan. 1, 1831.
+19 Milton, b. Dec. 8, 1810, d. Apr. 25, 1883, m. Hannah Passmore, May 21, 1835.

7 HENRY AND RACHEL (GORE) CORTRIGHT, issue:

 20 Mary P., b. Nov. 18, 1799, d. 1884, unm.
 21 Cynthia, b. Nov. 24, 1801, m. Ariel Rogers.
+22 Louisa, b. Dec. 2, 1803, m. Arthur Smith, Apr. 8, 1821.
+23 Katherine, b. Mar. 4, 1805, d. June, 1851, m. John Chapman Snow.
+24 Houghton, b. Apr. 19, 1808, d. Dec. 7, 1864, m. Sarah Ann Jones, Jan. 24, 1835.
+25 Frances, b. Aug. 15, 1809, d. May 5, 1873, m. George Cone, 1850.
 26 Sarah M., b. Dec. 29, 1811, d. Apr. 11, 1881, unm.
+27 Burton, b. Mar. 15, 1814, d. Jan. 10, 1888, m. Lucy Ann Larned, Dec. 19, 1838.
 28 Henry, Jr., b. July 21, 1817, d. Feb. 2, 1828.

8 JOHN AND MARY (ABBOTT) CORTRIGHT, issue:

+29 Hannah, b. June 9, 1801, d. Oct. 22, 1878, m. Horace G. Phelps, July 14, 1819.
+30 Cornelius, b. May 28, 1803, d. Sept. 7, 1894, m. Harriet Bailey, July 10, 1827.
+31 Roxanna, b. Oct. 12, 1805, d. Jan. 19, 1850, m. James M. Chamberlin, May 27, 1833.
+32 Charles A., b. Mar. 4, 1807, d. Sept. 12, 1856, m. Rebecca R. Hart, Feb. 19, 1829.
+33 John Draper, b. Dec. 29, 1808, d. Jan. 29, 1887, m. Hannah Rhodes, Sept. 27, 1843.
+34 Volney F., b. June 17, 1811, d. Aug. 19, 1855, m. Philena J. Hamlin, May 5, 1836.
+35 Eliza Ann, b. May 14, 1814, d. Sept. 20, 1845, m. George Cone, Dec. 6, 1831.

The above children were born in Plains Township, Luzerne County, Pa., near Wilkes Barre, and all of them wrote their name, Courtright, departing from the old style of their fathers.

EIGHTH GENERATION

9. MARY COURTRIGHT, born July 29, 1787, was baptized at the Reformed Dutch Church, at Machackemeck (Deerpark), Jan. 27, 1788, the daughter of Cornelius Cortright and Cattrina Cannady. She married John Murphy, who was a miller at Plains, when a young man, but who removed to Ohio at an early date, where he engaged in farming. They had issue:

+36   Sarah, b. Aug. 18, 1818, d. Apr. 11, 1855, m. Elias Cooper, Dec. 31, 1836.
+37   Elizabeth, b. Jan. 25, 1821, d. Nov. 5, 1883, m. Lewis Cooper, and m. 2d, Wellington Hurd, Mar. 18, 1851.
+38   Lucinda, b. Mar. 1, 1823, d. Jan. 4, 1886, m. Bentley S. Runyan, Jan. 14, 1844.
+39   Mary C., b. Dec. 18, 1825, d. Feb. 22, 1889, m. Robert Mead.

10. BENJAMIN COURTRIGHT, born Mar. 19, 1789, was baptized at Macheckemeck, July 3, 1789, his parents recorded as Cornelius Cortright and Caty Cannaday, by Rev. David Marenus. He was a farmer at Plains, where he spent his life, and married there Clarissa Williams, having issue:

+40   William Hamilton, b. Feb. 4, 1822, d. Feb. 15, 1902, m. Clara Swallow, Sept. 15, 1850, m. 2d, Mary A. Morgan, Oct. 25, 1864.
+41   Benjamin Franklin, b. May 31, 1826, d. Aug. 9, 1902, m. Annie L. Mitchell, May 28, 1860.
  42   John Milton, b. Sept. 12, 1828, d. Feb. 22, 1894, m. Mrs. Lydia Wanick, in 1863.
+43   James, b. Nov. 9, 1831, d. Dec. 8, 1914, m. Ruth Gore Searle, Sept. 19, 1854.
+44   Thomas W., b. July 22, 1834, d. Sept. 1, 1895, m. Elizabeth Mitchell, May 28, 1867.
+45   Mary E., b. Nov. 20, 1836, d. Mar. 20, 1912, m. Murray Breese, Oct. 26, 1858, m. 2d, John Sharps, Jan. 18, 1887.

11. CATHERINE COURTRIGHT, born Oct. 11, 1790, was baptized at Machackemeck, Nov. 1, 1790, her parents recorded as Cornelius Cortrecht and Cattrina Caneda, by Rev. David Marinus. She married Jan. 5, 1811, Isaiah Tyson, a miller at Plains, who with his family removed to Toronto, Canada, and very little known of them. So far as known, they had issue ·

  46   Joseph.
  47   Thomas.
  48   A dau. who m. —— Smith.
  49   A dau. who m. —— Lount.

12. JOHN COURTRIGHT, born Oct. 12, 1790, a twin with Catharine, was baptized at the same place and time she was. He was a farmer, married Lois Searle, Jan. 7, 1816, at Plains, and had issue ·

+50   George, b. Apr. 26, 1818, d. Feb. 28, 1903, m. Mary Mathers, Dec. 30, 1841.
 51   Cornelius, b. Dec. 3, 1820, m. Fidelia ——.
+52   Louisa S., b. Jan. 22, 1823, d. May 6, 1889, m. William Barnum, m. 2d, Davis H. Dotterer.
+53   Hannah, b. Apr. 15, 1825, m. Hamilton Stone.

13. HENRY COURTRIGHT, born Sept. 4, 1792, at Plains, was a farmer, and very little has been recovered concerning him. He married Sarah Bidleman, of Easton, Pa., and had issue:

+54   Elizabeth, b. Mar. 19, 1816, bap. at Wilkes Barre, Mar. 21, 1817, d. Sept. 28, 1868, m. John White, Aug. 2, 1835.
+55   Catharine, b. Mar. 19, 1819, m. Joseph Gardner.
 56   Rosanna, bap. at Wilkes Barre, Jan. 31, 1821.
+57   Margaret, b. Jan. 10, 1823, d. Nov. 30, 1882, m. George W. Barber, Mar. 2, 1842.
+58   Winfield S., b. Jan. 20, 1825, d. Nov. 10, 1892, m. Katherine Washburn.
+59   Mary, b. 1827, m. Henry F. Williams, m. 2d, Henry Mott.
 60   William B., b. Mar. 17, 1829, d. Dec. 26, 1898, m. Julia Reinsmith.
+61   Ellen, b. 1830, d. June 26, 1891, m. William K. Phillips.
+62   Charles W., b. Mar. 27, 1836, d. May 27, 1899, m. Frances Augusta Colby.
 63   Henry Harrison, b. Feb. 9, 1837, d. Oct. 11, 1901, m. Henrietta M. Burton, Aug. 20, 1860.

Henry H. Courtright, when a young man, entered the service of the Lehigh Railroad; came west and for several years was in the employ of the Chicago and Galena Railway; went to Hannibal, Mo., during the Civil War, where he was Agent for the Hannibal & St. Joseph Railway, and often made trips by coach to Santa Fe over the old trail. He later became General Freight Agent of the old Hannibal & St. Joseph Ry., and during the war, General Grant, at that time a Colonel, often used his office at Hannibal for his headquarters. For many years he was General Freight Agent of the Chicago and Alton Ry., located in Chicago, finally becoming chairman of the Western Freight Association.

He was a gentleman of the old school, of fine appearance, courtly bearing, kind and considerate to others, and in a quiet way dispensed charity to many needy families in Chicago. He had a great store of sentiment, was attached to his kindred, and took a great interest in the genealogy of his family, printing a small record of it, which contained all there was available at the time. This tribute to his memory is from one who had the greatest respect and affection for him.

15. HANNAH COURTRIGHT, born at Plains, Feb. 7, 1798, just outside the present limits of Wilkes Barre, Luzerne County, Pa., married John Abbott, a farmer at Plains March 11, 1830, and died May 3, 1892, having attained the extreme old age of over ninety-four years.

At the time of her birth, Wilkes Barre was only a little hamlet in a great wilderness, and she vividly recalled many a ride from her home at Plains to Wilkes Barre, either alone, or on horse-back with her father.

She also remembered well hearing the survivors of the Wyoming massacre tell about that bloody event, for many of them were alive during her recollection—the terrors inspired by the presence of the savages, the eager hanging of the women and children upon the Gospel Minister to shield and protect them, the merciless attack of the British and Indians, the flight across the mountains through the "shades of death" to the Minisink settlements or to Connecticutt, the sufferings of the almost naked children, the birth of a child during this mad stampede and the tender efforts of the fugitives to provide for the mother and carry her on blankets fastened to two horses—these and many other incidents were familiar tales to her.

It was hard for her to realize the changes since the old days, the telephone, the telegraph, the electric cars, and many other modern improvements. When speaking of the electric cars, she said they reminded her of lines that ran through her mind, where taken from, not known, "the arm of Omnipotent power they assume, and ride in chariots of fire." certainly not an unprophetic description.

She was a consistent member of the Methodist church for eighty years, having become a member thereof at the age of fourteen, and throughout her life she was comforted by a faith which never wavered. She was a woman of wonderful energy, of rugged constitution, and up to two years previous to her death, her faculties were unimpaired and at the time of her death, she was the oldest person in Luzerne County.

Soon after the death of her husband in 1861, she removed with her children from her home at Plains, and thereafter resided on the corner of Franklin and Jackson Streets, Wilkes Barre, Pa.

John and Hannah (Courtright) Abbott had issue:

64 Robert, b. Aug. 25, 1831, d. July 10, 1836.
65 Lucy Waller, b. Nov. 25, 1833, d. Dec. 3, 1914, unm.

+66   Robert Miner, b. June 15, 1836, m. Caroline A. Courtright, Dec. 29, 1864, d. Apr. 14, 1922.

67   Catharine C., b. Dec. 16, 1838, d. Apr. 8, 1894, unm.

17. ELEANOR COURTRIGHT, born at Plains, Sept. 13, 1804, married William Abbott, Nov. 2, 1824, died Mar. 10, 1886. They went to Knox County, Ohio, at an early day, where her husband bought a large farm near Mt. Vernon, where they continued to reside during their lives.

They had issue:

+68   John Sommerfield, b. June 16, 1825, d. Dec. 23, 1903, m. Mary Emeline Johnson, Feb. 15, 1866.

69   Lucinda Courtright, b. Sept. 22, 1826, d. Jan. 30, 1861, m. Lorenzo Adams, m. 2d, David Mead

70   Stephen, b. Sept. 25, 1830, d. Jan. 19, 1866, m. Mary Saylor.

71   Cornelius Courtright, b. Jan. 22, 1833.

18. ELIZABETH COURTRIGHT, born at Plains, June 25, 1807, married Charles Miner Wright, Jan 1, 1831, and d. 1890. They had issue:

+73   Milton C., b. Oct. 10, 1834, m. Julia Edgerton, Mar. 17, 1862, m. 2d, Adah J. Shumaker, July 9, 1873, m. 3d, Margaret Ownsby, Sept. 19, 1883.

74   Mary, b. Dec. 4, 1837, d. Apr. 9, 1864, m. James Rowe, Dec. 4, 1861.

+75   Josiah, b. May 10, 1839, d. June 21, 1921, m. Mary Edgerton, Aug. 11, 1870.

+76   Josephine, b. Jan. 31, 1845, m. Benjamin B. Courtright, Feb. 9, 1870.

+77   Charles F., b. July 5, 1853, d. Aug. 4, 1916, m. Margaret Farmer, Oct. 20, 1883.

19. MILTON COURTRIGHT, born Dec. 8, 1810, at Plains, married Hannah Passmore, May 21, 1835, and died Apr. 25, 1883. He was an Alumnus of Gambier College, Knox County, Ohio, a civil engineer by profession, and removed to New York, where he introduced rapid transit, and was first president of the elevated road there. He was the builder of the Canada Southern, now the Michigan Central Railroad, also its president, and became wealthy and prominent. They had issue:

78   Norman Passmore, b. in 1836, d. 1877.

+79   Catherine Elizabeth, b. May 9, 1838, m. Col. Reigert B. Lowry, Oct. 6, 1857, m. 2d, Eben Brewer, Dec. 14, 1882.

+80   John Milton, b. Feb. 7, 1841, d. June 27, 1873, m. Fanny Badger, 1863.

81   Louise Deshler, b. about 1845, d. young.

+82   Hannah Alice, b. Mar. 14, 1852, d. Mar. 1, 1911, m. Dr. Richard K. Valentine, Nov. 21, 1883.

22. Louisa Courtright, born Dec. 2, 1803, married Arthur Smith, April 8, 1821, having issue:

  83   Stephen Henry, b. Jan. 30, 1822, d. Apr. 5, 1849.
  84   Welthy Ann, b. Dec. 20, 1824, d. June 27, 1827.
  85   Ruth Ann, b. May 7, 1828, d. Jan. 22, 1833.
+86   Louisa, b. May 27, 1830, d. Aug. 14, 1862, m. Dunham Lamb, Mar. 29, 1852.
  87   Frances L., b. Oct. 19, 1841, d. Apr. 27, 1857.

23. Katherine Courtright, born Mar. 4, 1805, d. June, 1851, married John Chapman Snow, having issue:

  88   Mary E., no record.
+89   Joseph C., b. Apr. 1, 1835, d. Jan. 17, 1916, m. Elizabeth Getzler, Sept. 24, 1860.
  90   Louise F., b. Oct. 9, 1836, d. Feb. 3, 1916, m. John F. Quin.
  91   Katherine H., b. May 7, 1846, d. Apr. 8, 1914.

24. Houghton Courtright, born Apr. 19, 1808, married Sarah A. Jones, Jan. 24, 1835, died Dec. 7, 1864, a farmer, had issue ·

  93   Sarah Elizabeth, b. Aug. 20, 1837, m. Horatio Mulford, June 30, 1859.
+94   Henry, b. Dec. 15, 1840, d. Dec. 24, 1903, m. Nancy Jackson, Jan. 4, 1864.
+95   Meredith J., b. Dec. 11, 1859, d. Mar. 20, 1922, m. Cora E. Shelly, Apr. 20, 1886.

Houghton Courtright had several other children, who died young.

25. Frances L. Courtright, born Aug. 15, 1809, married George Cone, and died May 5, 1873, had issue:

+96   Mary L., b. Jan. 3, 1857, m. Rev. Luther R. Steele, May 11, 1876.

27. Burton Courtright, born Mar. 15, 1814, married Lucy Ann Larned, Dec. 19, 1838, and died Jan. 10, 1888, a farmer, had issue:

+97   Mary C., b. July 4, 1840, d. Aug. 3, 1886, m. Stephen D. Lewis, Dec. 3, 1865.
  98   Adelaide C., b. 1841, d. Aug. 25, 1904, unm.
+99   Oscar L., b. Aug. 6, 1842, m. Sophia Stephens, Apr. 5, 1865.
+100 Seymour, b. July 29, 1845, d. Nov. 13, 1916, m. Harriet E. Heft, July 4, 1874, m. 2d, Emma Phoenix, Mar. 31, 1892.
+101 Everett B., b. Feb. 13, 1849, d. Feb. 4, 1907, m. Elizabeth Posten, Mar. 7, 1875.
+102 Frank, b. Aug. 9, 1854, d. Apr. 22, 1897, m. Ida Posten, Feb. 28, 1880.
  103 Alice G., b. Sept. 22, 1860, m. Riter T. Smith, July 3, 1912.

29. HANNAH COURTRIGHT, born June 9, 1801, married Horace G. Phelps, July 14, 1819, and died Oct. 22, 1878, had issue:

  104   John C., b. May 8, 1822, d. Jan. 27, 1887, m. Sarah Stevens, June 6, 1852.

+105   Mary E., b. Sept. 22, 1824, d. Sept. 26, 1914, m. Claudius B. Pratt, Oct. 12, 1846.

  106   Elisha, b. Apr. 12, 1827, d. July, 1851.

+107   Legrand D., b. Jan. 9, 1829, d. Dec. 24, 1890, m. Mary Hendrick, Aug. 14, 1855.

+108   Martha, b. Apr. 3, 1834, d. Mar. 22, 1917, m. Alonzo H. Terwilliger, Dec. 6, 1859.

  109   Horace B., b. May 11, 1843, d. Nov. 21, 1881, m. Mary E. Throop, June 20, 1866.

30. CORNELIUS L. COURTRIGHT, born at Plains, Luzerne County, Pa., May 28, 1803, married Harriet Bailey, July 10, 1827, and died Sept. 7, 1894, was a farmer, who with his brother, John Draper, inherited the ancestral farm at Plains, and which they operated for several years.

Afterward he engaged in the contracting business, building a canal along the Susquehanna River, and in 1833, he employed more than 300 men on public work in Virginia, but owing to the cholera, causing the death of half his men, and also afflicted himself, he was unable to complete the work he had undertaken. He later took contracts to convey pine lumber and arks of coal down the Susquehanna River and Chesapeake Bay to Baltimore, which he successfully accomplished.

He returned to his farm at Plains, residing there for a time, but on May 27, 1839, hearing glowing accounts of cheap lands in the west, he sold his farm, not knowing the value of the coal underneath, and with his wife and children, departed in a covered wagon to Detroit, by boat to Chicago, then but a small village, and settled on a farm which he bought near Newark, Kendall County, Illinois, where he lived until death, having attained the ripe age of ninety-one years.

After the death of his wife, he married Mrs. Susanna Luther, July 4, 1852, who survived him several years. He was a man of the highest character, honest, industrious, of sterling qualities, and had the respect and esteem of his friends and neighbors. By his first wife, he had issue:

+110   Louisa P., b. Jan. 27, 1829, d. Sept. 30, 1915, m. Thomas J. Phillips, Feb. 15, 1844.

+111   John Milton, b. Aug. 6, 1830, d. June 8, 1901, m. Margaret T. Rhodes, Apr. 12, 1855, m. 2d, Sarah C. Diffenbacher, Sept. 25, 1860, m. 3d, Susan L. Olney, July, 9, 1878.

+112   Roxanna, b. Sept. 8, 1832, m. J. Henry Pierce, June 22, 1858, m. 2d, James H. Huntoon, Dec. 3, 1872, m. 3d, Peter Misner, Apr. 15, 1887.

+113   Horace P., b. Aug. 18, 1834, d. Jan. 6, 1922, m. Phoebe A. Cook, Oct. 23, 1858.

+114   Lydia B., b. June 13, 1836, d. Jan. 24, 1922, m. John Ruble, Nov. 28, 1852.

+115   Benjamin B., b. Aug. 12, 1838, d. Dec. 13, 1915, m. Josephine Wright, Feb. 9, 1870.

+116   Harriet A., b. Oct. 17, 1840, m. Peter S. Mackay, Sept. 18, 1862.

+117   Caroline A., b. Nov. 4, 1842, m. Robert Miner Abbott, Dec. 29, 1864.

+118   Cornelius C., b. Sept. 19, 1844, m. Anna Newton, Sept. 10, 1868.

+119   Charles O., b. Jan. 30, 1847, d. Oct. 5, 1915, m. Jennie Fairfield, Sept. 23, 1875.

+120   Chester O., b. Mar. 28, 1849, d. June 13, 1910, m. Ada M. Haskins, Dec. 23, 1880.

31. ROXANNA COURTRIGHT, born Oct. 12, 1805, married James M. Chamberlin, May 27, 1833, died Jan. 19, 1850, had issue:

+121   John Wilson, b. May 21, 1837, d. Aug. 11, 1901, m. Mary T. Cowles, June 6, 1861, m. 2d, Livonia R. Buell, Nov. 2, 1870.

32. CHARLES A. COURTRIGHT, born Mar. 4, 1807, d. Sept. 12, 1856, married Rebecca R. Hart, Feb. 19, 1829, had issue:

122   Sarah L., b. Feb. 7, 1830, d. Feb. 3, 1855.

+123   Ruth A., b. June 23, 1833, d. Aug. 2, 1910, m. Carlton O. Lee, Feb. 28, 1871.

+124   Horace P., b. May 17, 1838, d. Feb. 17, 1914, m. Mary E. Pollard, Sept. 26, 1871.

+125   Mary E., b. Aug. 24, 1849, m. Joseph A. Bigger, Mar. 12, 1878.

33. JOHN DRAPER COURTRIGHT, born Dec. 27, 1808, married Hannah Rhodes Sept. 27, 1843, died Jan. 29, 1887, was born on the farm of his father at Plains, Pa., which he inherited jointly with his brother Cornelius, and on which he resided for several years. Later he sold his interest in this farm and removed to a farm near Sheridan, Illinois, (not far from that of his brother Cornelius), his future home. Their issue:

+126   Milton Le Grand, b. Nov. 5, 1844, m. Emma E. Ford, Dec. 24, 1868.

+127   Mary Leonora, b. Apr. 27, 1846, d. Sept. 29, 1902, m. John C. Van Natta, Oct. 2, 1884.

128   Ellen Josephine, b. Aug. 16, 1857, m. Thomas B. McLean, June 10, 1895.

34. VOLNEY COURTRIGHT, born June 17, 1811, married Philena J. Hamlin, May 5, 1836, died Aug. 19, 1855, had issue:

+129   Chancy A., b. Mar. 10, 1837, d. Dec. 23, 1920, m. Lizzie Battin, Oct. 6, 1864.

130   Eugene B., b. Sept. 14, 1838, d. Feb. 8, 1863.

+131   Mary S., b. Feb. 10, 1841, d. Aug. 17, 1917, m. Edward A. Forrester, Feb. 12, 1868.

+·132   Eliza A., b. Sept. 1, 1842, d. Dec. 14, 1916, m. Thomas J. Megargel, Feb. 28, 1872.

+133   George C., b. Sept. 14, 1844, m. Anna E. Luce, Sept. 9, 1874.

134   Utley Abbott, b. Jan. 28, 1847, d. Feb. 2, 1869.

+135   Martha H., b. Jan. 22, 1851, d. Mar. 6, 1917, m. Lorenzo D. Kemmerer, May 13, 1874.

35. ELIZA ANN COURTRIGHT, born May 4, 1814, died Sept. 20, 1845, married George Cone, Dec. 6, 1831, and had issue:

136   Hannah R., b. Aug. 21, 1833, d. Oct. 30, 1902, m. J. Edward Lent, Aug. 26, 1858.

+137   Dorastus, b. Dec. 17, 1836, d. May 30, 1885, m. Martha R. Lacey, Sept. 7, 1858.

NINTH GENERATION

36 ELIAS AND SARAH (MURPHY) COOPER, issue:

138   James, b. July 9, 1838, d. July 18, 1838.

139   Ellen, b. Sept. 5, 1840, d. Jan. 5, 1843.

+140   Mary, b. Oct. 4, 1841, m. Col. George Rogers.

+141   Charles G., b. Dec. 11, 1845, m. Carrie Cady, Sept. 1, 1874, and m. 2d, Irene Martin, Sept. 24, 1900.

37 WELLINGTON AND ELIZABETH (MURPHY) HURD, issue:

+142   Wellington E., b. June 14, 1852, d. Nov. 17, 1908, m. Anna Eliza Brooks, 1882, m. 2d, Julia Moffitt, 1890.

+143   Louie L., b. Apr. 15, 1855, d. June 22, 1917, m. Fred J. Reese, Dec. 24, 1883.

+144   Mary E., b. Aug. 14, 1858, m. Addis A. Cannon, Nov. 20, 1884.

145   Anson, b. July 11, 1860.

+146   Charles J., b. Apr. 13, 1862, m. Nellie Crane, Apr. 10, 1889.

38 BENTLEY S. AND LUCINDA (MURPHY) RUNYAN, issue:

+147   John B., b. Feb. 9, 1846, d. June 6, 1906, m. Charlotte Hedges, Oct. 12, 1870.

+148   Charles C., b. Nov. 1, 1848, d. Oct. 8, 1915, m. Tina R. Wright, Nov. 5, 1870.

149   Robert M., b. Feb. 9, 1851, d. Sept. 24, 1852.

+150   Mead, b. Jan. 15, 1853, d. Dec. 16, 1914, m. Ida Boyle, Jan. 20, 1875.

+151   Almeda, b. May 20, 1855, m. Uel R. Parsons, Oct. 10, 1883.

152   Mary Ellen, b. May 2, 1859.

39 ROBERT AND MARY C. (MURPHY) MEAD, issue:

+153   Sadie, b. Sept. 23, 1852, m. Willis M. Sturges, Feb. 5, 1879.

154   Mamie, b. about 1855, d. young.

40 WILLIAM HAMILTON AND CLARA (SWALLOW) COURTRIGHT, issue:

155 Josephine Estella, b. July 17, 1851, d. Apr. 21, 1873.
156 Benjamin Rush, b. June 25, 1853, m. Lina Goble, Apr. 12, 1888.
+157 Joseph Miner, b. June 19, 1859, m. Joanna Goble, June 16, 1894.
+158 Elizabeth, b. Nov. 14, 1861, m. James Wentz, Dec. 18, 1884.

40 WILLIAM HAMILTON AND MARY A. (MORGAN) COURTRIGHT, issue·

159 William Arthur, b. Aug. 30, 1866, m. Nellie A. Morehead, Nov. 14, 1889.
+160 Gertrude, b. Mar. 22, 1873, m. George B. Windsor, Mar. 22, 1892.
161 Nellie, b. Oct. 7, 1879, d. Oct. 18, 1897.
+162 Lillian Pearl, b. June 7, 1884, m. William Herbert Lee, June 30, 1907.
+163 Milton Roy, b. Feb. 26, 1890, m. May Groteguth, Aug. 18, 1915.

41 BENJAMIN FRANKLIN AND ANNIE (MITCHELL) COURTRIGHT, issue:

+164 Isabelle, b. May 5, 1862, m. William V. Good, Dec. 28, 1887.
+165 Clara R., b. July 20, 1864, m. Dr. Granville T. Matlack, Apr. 5, 1888.
+166 John M., b. May 9, 1866, m. Kate (Daniels) Stuckey, Sept. 2, 1904.
167 Murray B., b. Jan. 9, 1868, m. Louise Matlack, Sept. 2, 1914.
+168 Jennie N., b. Aug. 10, 1869, m. Charles Sheldon, Dec. 29, 1896.
169 Mae A., b. Mar. 30, 1871.
170 Archibald O., b. July 20, 1875.
+171 William W., b. Sept. 14, 1881, m. Reba Henderson, Aug. 28, 1905.

43 JAMES AND RUTH GORE (SEARLE) COURTRIGHT, issue:

+172 John Searle, b. July 21, 1855, m. Ellen Lathrop, Jan. 17, 1877.
+173 Harrie B., b. Feb. 18, 1857, d. May 15, 1910, m. Clara Ida Wells, Mar. 7, 1876.

44 THOMAS W. AND ELIZABETH (MITCHELL) COURTRIGHT, issue:

+174 George R., b. July 10, 1869, m. Mary A. Coy, Jan. 1, 1892.
175 Florence L., b. June 20, 1872.
+176 Mary E., b. Feb. 10, 1876, m. Wilbert W. Lamb, Nov. 5, 1911.
177 Lena B., b. Dec. 6, 1878.
178 Helen B., b. Oct. 4, 1881.
179 Benjamin F., b. May 8, 1885, m. Zada Imboden, Oct. 2, 1913.

45 MURRAY AND MARY E. (COURTRIGHT) BREESE, issue:

180 Clara Estelle, b. May 18, 1860, m. Draper Campbell, Apr. 18, 1884, m. 2d, John Calvin Bell, June 18, 1904.

+181   Jessie Falla, b. July 21, 1862, m. Homer P. Snyder, June 27, 1882.
+182   James Milton, b. Jan. 31, 1864, m. Grace Murray, Apr. 9, 1889.
183   Frank Murray, b. Sept. 21, 1871, d. Mar. 13, 1877.
184   Josephine C., b. Sept. 23, 1874, d. Apr. 1, 1877.

50 GEORGE AND MARY (MATHERS) COURTRIGHT, issue:

185   Mary Louise, b. Jan. 18, 1843, d. Oct. 9, 1868, m. William Shook.
+186   James M., b. Aug. 8, 1845, d. June 2, 1917, m. Gertrude Saleno, Dec. 21, 1882.
+187   John P., b. Aug. 17, 1847, d. July 7, 1918, m. Mary J. Mc Walters, Feb., 1877.
+188   William B., b. Feb. 1, 1850, d. Dec. 19, 1919, m. Louisa J. Hawley, Feb. 1, 1877.
+189   Lillian Fidelia, b. Oct. 4, 1859, m. John E. Nugent, Oct. 26, 1880.

52 WILLIAM AND LOUISA (COURTRIGHT) BARNUM, issue:

+190   Dellie, m. James Verplank.

52 DAVIS H. AND LOUISA (COURTRIGHT) DOTTERER, issue:

+191   Louise, b. Feb., 1857, d. Mar. 4, 1897, m. John Wolford Mumper, Sept. 22, 1879.
192   William C., b. Apr. 9, 1859.

53 HAMILTON AND HANNAH (COURTRIGHT) STONE, issue:

+193   Mollie, m. James Hancock.
194   Hattie.
195   William.

54 JOHN AND ELIZABETH (COURTRIGHT) WHITE, issue:

+196   Henry C., b. July 2, 1836, d. Dec. 28, 1892, m. Sarah Butz, Dec. 15, 1863.
+197   Sarah E., b. July 16, 1844, d. 1876, m. Norman Tracy.
+198   Margaret B., b. June 2, 1848, m. Harry S. Gilchrist, May 1, 1877.
199   Charles A., b. Jan. 19, 1850.
200   Joshua L., b. Dec. 9, 1859, d. young.

55 JOSEPH AND CATHARINE (COURTRIGHT) GARDNER, issue:

201   Harry.

57 GEORGE W. AND MARGARET (COURTRIGHT) BARBER, issue:

+202   Helen Rosanna, b. Mar. 7, 1843, d. Jan. 24, 1867, m. John S. Lazarus, Nov. 1, 1863.
+203   Joseph B., b. Mar. 12, 1845, m. Anna E. Benford, Sept. 14, 1870.
204   Charles Weyl, b. Jan. 26, 1848, d. Feb. 24, 1868.
+205   Mary Margaret, b. May 28, 1850, m. James H. Runyon, Feb. 12, 1874.
206   Catharine Louise, b. Dec. 6, 1852, d. July 30, 1863.
207   William Courtright, b. May 24, 1855, d. July 14, 1880.

208 Emma Gertrude, b. Jan. 10, 1858, m. Thomas A. Garrigues, Aug. 26, 1896.

+209 Elizabeth Sarah, b. Apr. 9, 1860, m. William T. Phillips, Sept. 9, 1884.

+210 Henry Harrison, b. Oct. 24, 1863, d. Nov. 26, 1897, m. Dove M. Foster, Aug. 31, 1889.

211 Benjamin Franklin, b. Dec. 24, 1865, d. Apr. 5, 1881.

58 WINFIELD S. AND KATHERINE (WASHBURN) COURTRIGHT, issue:

212 Carrie M., b. Apr. 4, 1845, d. young.

213 William W., b. May 6, 1847, d. young.

214 Harry M., b. May 10, 1850, d. young.

59 HENRY F. AND MARY (COURTRIGHT) WILLIAMS, issue:

+215 Rose C., b. May 11, 1849, d. Feb. 20, 1892, m. Judson S. Stark, Sept. 29, 1868.

+216 John W., b. Apr. 8, 1853, m. Elizabeth Studley.

59 HENRY AND MARY (COURTRIGHT) MOTT, issue:

+217 Chester B., b. Jan. 29, 1859, m. Anna E. Martin, July 21, 1892.

+218 Ida, b. June 2, 1863, m. Benage S. Josselyn, Apr. 15, 1885.

61 WILLIAM K. AND ELLEN (COURTRIGHT) PHILLIPS, issue:

+219 Isadore, b. Sept. 2, 1856, d. Feb. 19, 1916, m. Morris A. McClenthen, Sept., 1876.

220 Clara C., b. Oct. 6, 1858, m. Henry Langdon, Nov. 29, 1895.

+221 Herman F., b. Dec. 13, 1863, m. Ada L. Roll, Sept. 5, 1887.

+222 Winfield C., b. Nov. 13, 1864, m. Bertha Strong, Feb. 17, 1886, m. 2d, Dora B. Rivers, Feb. 27, 1890.

+223 G. Harding, b. Feb. 5, 1874, m. Ida J. Rhinefield, Apr. 26, 1892.

62 CHARLES W. AND FRANCES A. (COLBY) COURTRIGHT, issue:

224 Edward W., b. Mar. 11, 1869, d. 1901.

225 Helen Imogen, b. Aug. 17, 1877, m. Emil J. Munkwitz, Jan. 12, 1904.

66 ROBERT MINER AND CAROLINE A. (COURTRIGHT) ABBOTT, issue:

226 John Howard, b. Feb. 26, 1866, m. Mabel G. Hax, June 2, 1913.

227 Carrie Helene, b. Nov. 22, 1867, m. Ira R. Tabor, Nov. 22, 1910.

228 Robert Bruce, b. Aug. 18, 1873, m. Teckla Engburgh, Dec. 29, 1914, m. 2d, Cora A. Engburgh, June 21, 1919.

68 JOHN SOMMERFIELD AND MARY E. (JOHNSON) ABBOTT, issue:

+229 Lulu Courtright, b. Dec. 7, 1866, m. Burton D. Herron, Aug. 23, 1902.

73 MILTON C. AND JULIA (EDGERTON) WRIGHT, issue:

230 Estella, b. Mar. 10, 1867, m. William J. Saltmarsh, Oct. 22, 1895.
231 Chester, b. Jan. 20, 1869, m. Rosa Saltmarsh, Feb. 26, 1896.

73 MILTON C. AND ADAH J. (SHUMAKER) WRIGHT, issue:

+232 George, b. July 5, 1876, m. Mayme Johnson, Aug. 16, 1902.
233 Mary Pearl, b. Jan. 28, 1883, d. Sept. 28, 1919, m. Fred Shores, Sept. 14, 1904.

73 MILTON C. AND MARGARET (OWNSBY) WRIGHT, issue:

234 Albert O., b. Dec. 18, 1891, m. Juanita Ryan, Nov. 8, 1911.

75 JOSIAH AND MARY (EDGERTON) WRIGHT, issue:

+235 Minnie E., b. June 23, 1871, m. Arthur P. Twichell, Oct. 13, 1892.

76 BENJAMIN B. AND JOSEPHINE (WRIGHT) COURTRIGHT, issue:

236 Ella J., b. Oct. 5, 1871, d. Feb. 23, 1890.
+237 Jessie E., b. Nov. 29, 1872, m. Edward Larson, Nov. 29, 1891.
238 Evangeline, b. Sept. 25, 1874, m. Albert N. Parker, May 5, 1894.
+239 Mabel C., b. Sept. 12, 1876, m. Maitland Hill, June 14, 1906.
+240 Winfred M., b. Oct. 8, 1878, m. Grace V. Wing, Oct. 18, 1906.
241 Chester A., b. Jan. 12, 1881.
+242 Gaylord M., b. Dec. 27, 1886, m. Nelle M. Boyd, Sept. 5, 1916.
+243 Guy B., b. Dec. 27, 1886, m. Georgia Miller, Dec. 2, 1915.
+244 Charlotte, b. Mar. 23, 1891, m. Alexander R. Thompson, Sept. 29, 1914.

77 CHARLES F. AND MARGARET (FARMER) WRIGHT, issue:

245 Edward, b. Aug. 28, 1903.

79 COL. REIGERT B. AND CATHERINE ELIZABETH (COURTRIGHT) LOWRY, issue:

+246 Ricardo St. P., b. Feb. 25, 1864, d. Aug. 14, 1919, m. Annie Wrenton Maus, Oct. 17, 1888.
+247 Walter C., b. Nov. 16, 1865, m. Margaret C. Griffin, Dec. 29, 1890.
248 Marion, b. Feb. 11, 1869, d. July 5, 1919, m. Col. Frank Michler, Jan., 1900, m. 2d, Frederick S. Minot, Feb. 11, 1906.
249 Robert Oliver, b. Aug. 3, 1870, d. Nov. 16, 1895.

80 JOHN MILTON AND FANNY (BADGER) COURTRIGHT, issue:

250 William B., b. Sept. 25, 1864.
251 Louisa N., b. May 14, 1866, d. July 27, 1920, m. Frank D. Fearman, Apr. 17, 1909.

82 DR. RICHARD K. AND HANNAH A. (COURTRIGHT) VALENTINE, issue:

252 Milton C., b. Sept. 17, 1884, d. Feb. 12, 1889.

253 Richard K., b. Nov. 25, 1887, m. Elizabeth Browning, Feb. 20, 1915.

86 DUNHAM AND LOUISA (SMITH) LAMB, issue:

+254 Alice E., b. Sept. 14, 1853, m. William B. Keller, Feb. 15, 1883.
255 Arthur D., b. May 17, 1858, d. July 9, 1858.
256 Walter, b. Apr. 22, 1860, d. Aug. 14, 1860.

89 JOSEPH C. AND ELIZABETH (GETZLER) SNOW, issue:

257 Harry W., b. May 20, 1862, d. Jan. 13, 1892.
258 George W., b. Sept. 17, 1863, d. young.
259 Arthur M., b. Oct. 7, 1864, d. young.
260 Frank C., b. Aug. 7, 1866.
+261 Ellen H., b. Sept. 17, 1869, m. Charles D. Hawn, Nov. 18, 1891.
+262 Maud J., b. Dec. 9, 1872, m. Charles A. Foley, Oct. 21, 1896.
263 Joseph C., b. Feb. 27, 1875, d. young.
+264 Burton C., b. July 14, 1878, m. Ethel M. Kelly, June 7, 1905.

94 HENRY AND NANCY (JACKSON) COURTRIGHT, issue:

+265 Lillian, b. Apr. 2, 1865, m. Frank B. Thompson, Nov. 14, 1883.
+266 Benjamin, b. Dec. 30, 1866, m. Charity M. Smith, Dec. 15, 1895.
267 Alonzo J., b. Apr. 28, 1868.
268 Rosamond, b. Jan. 15, 1870, d. May 16, 1919.
+269 Harriet, b. Oct. 9, 1871, m. Oliver R. Moore, Aug. 29, 1890.
270 Horatio H., b. Sept. 1876, d. May 4, 1920.
+271 Elizabeth M., b. Mar. 18, 1881, m. Edward T. Evans, May 9, 1900.

95 MEREDITH J. AND CORA E. (SHELLY) COURTRIGHT, issue:

272 Edna, b. Jan. 7, 1889, m. J. Homer Greggs, Oct. 19, 1920.
273 Ruth, b. Mar. 14, 1894, d. Dec. 28, 1899.

96 REV. LUTHER R. AND MARY L. (CONE) STEELE, issue:

274 Frances C., b. Nov. 23, 1878, m. Edward A. Burdette, Oct. 9, 1909.
275 John H., b. Dec. 13, 1880, d. Feb. 20, 1901.
276 Spencer C., b. Sept. 27, 1883, d. May 21, 1889.
277 Mary C., b. Dec. 9, 1889, m. Charles S. Suraci, Aug. 12, 1912.

97 STEPHEN D. AND MARY C. (COURTRIGHT) LEWIS, issue:

+278 Oscar C., b. Jan. 31, 1866, m. Laura Bailey, June 11, 1890.
+279 Frances E., b. Oct. 18, 1867, m. Walter A. Lewis, Dec. 24, 1888.
+280 Everett B., b. Feb. 26, 1871, m. Estelle Flagler, June 30, 1894.
+281 Alice L., b. May 25, 1877, m. Cornelius W. Hooghouse, Dec. 24, 1894.
+282 Blanche E., b. May 8, 1883, m. Leroy Stines, May 4, 1911.

99 OSCAR L. AND SOPHIA (STEPHENS) COURTRIGHT, issue:

283 Lewis S., b. June 30, 1870, d. June 23, 1883.

+284   Laura A., b. Oct. 9, 1866, d. Sept. 11, 1920, m. Lester Hough, Nov. 19, 1896.
285   Everett P., b. Oct. 12, 1868, d. June 28, 1916, m. Effie Anderson, Nov. 15, 1904.

100 SEYMOUR AND HARRIET E. (HEFT) COURTRIGHT, issue:
286   Alice L., b. Jan. 10, 1876, d. July 12, 1899, m. Robert Eaton, Apr., 1895.

100 SEYMOUR AND EMMA (PHOENIX) COURTRIGHT, issue:
287   Mona L., b. July 6, 1893.
288   Marion D., b. June 18, 1895.
289   Lucy A., b. June 4, 1898.

101 EVERETT B. AND ELIZABETH (POSTEN) COURTRIGHT, issue:
+290   Archie B., b. Jan. 14, 1879, d. Nov. 16, 1920, m. Bertha Morgan, Oct. 2, 1916.

102 FRANK AND IDA (POSTEN) COURTRIGHT, issue:
291   Burton A., b. Oct. 23, 1881, m. Marie Damon, Apr. 15, 1902.
⊥292   Nina M., b. Mar. 4, 1886, m. Albert W. Gabriel, June 18, 1913.

105 CLAUDIUS B. AND MARY E. (PHELPS) PRATT, issue·
+293   Mary E., b. Dec. 8, 1849, m. Samuel H. Stevens, May 21, 1873.
+294   Louise B., b. Nov. 23, 1851, m. William B. Henwood, Oct. 30, 1877.
+295   Leonora, b. Mar. 30, 1861, m. James L. Connell, Apr. 17, 1883.
+296   Claudius B., b. Jan. 30, 1864, d. Feb. 12, 1919, m. Helen Wagner, June 24, 1891.

107 LE GRAND D. AND MARY A. (HENDRICK) PHELPS, issue:
+297   Mary Alice, b. Apr. 14, 1858, m. James P. Crossley, Oct. 28, 1874.
+298   Horace G., b. Dec. 24, 1860, d. Dec. 5, 1912, m. Mary A. O'Shea, Apr. 4, 1885.
+299   Floy H., b. June 11, 1868, m. Frank J. Dignon, Apr. 15, 1888, m. 2d, William A. Lotti, Apr. 1, 1902.
+300   Jennie C., b. July 8, 1873, m. Albert B. Corcilius, Mar. 16, 1892.

108 ALONZO H. AND MARTHA (PHELPS) TERWILLIGER, issue:
301   Charles P., b. May 24, 1865.
302   Nellie S., b. Feb. 12, 1868.

110 THOMAS J. AND LOUISA P. (COURTRIGHT) PHILLIPS, issue:
303   Jefferson, b. July 27, 1845, d. Feb. 18, 1850.
304   Quincy, b. Mar. 29, 1848, d. Aug. 17, 1849.
+305   Carson E., b. July 3, 1851, m. Minnie L. Bennett, Oct. 10, 1883.
306   Ida Roxanna, b. June 21, 1854, m. Sylvanus Fowler, Jan. 13, 1875.

+307 Leslie S., b. Aug. 12, 1856, d. Mar. 26, 1898, m. Sadie A. Davison, Oct. 30, 1877.

308 T. Leland, b. Mar. 4, 1858, d. Dec. 13, 1920, m. Ida M. Lott, Aug. 26, 1884.

309 Carrie, b. Aug. 6, 1860, d. Sept. 12, 1861.

+310 Minnie J., b. Sept. 14, 1862, d. Nov. 26, 1904, m. J. Channing Seaton, Sept. 14, 1881.

+311 Mary Louise, b. Apr. 1, 1867, m. Alfred E. Harding, Oct. 22, 1884.

312 Charles B., b. Jan. 6, 1870, m. Clara A. Dubrock, June 24, 1896.

111 JOHN MILTON AND MARGARET T. (RHODES) COURTRIGHT, issue:

313 William, b. Nov. 9, 1856, d. Sept. 11, 1858.

+314 Charles Sigel, b. June 2, 1859, m. Anna M. Schlampp, Sept. 15, 1887.

111 JOHN MILTON AND SARAH C. (DIFFENBACHER) COURT-RIGHT, issue:

+315 Lillian N., b. Jan. 15, 1864, d. July 29, 1921, m. Albert W. Arnold, Dec. 23, 1886.

+316 Myrtle R., b. Sept. 28, 1867, d. June 16, 1914, m. Elmer F. Coddington, July 4, 1885.

112 J. HENRY AND ROXANNA (COURTRIGHT) PIERCE, issue:

317 Frank L., b. Dec. 3, 1860, d. Dec. 23, 1887.

318 William H., b. June 18, 1862, d. Sept. 11, 1883.

113 HORACE P. AND PHOEBE A. (COOK) COURTRIGHT, issue:

+319 Alonzo E., b. Mar. 1, 1861, m. Clara V. Wunder, Aug. 20, 1882.

+320 Harry M., b. Mar. 25, 1869, m. Mollie G. Shafter, Sept. 17, 1888.

114 JOHN AND LYDIA B. (COURTRIGHT) RUBLE, issue:

+321 Hattie L., b. June 9, 1860, m. Oscar W. Brown, Mar. 24, 1880, m. 2d, John Canham, Dec. 5, 1901.

+322 Carrie L., b. Aug. 16, 1862, m. Louis Weeks, Nov. 19, 1882.

323 Charles M., b. Apr. 18, 1866, d. June 1, 1866.

+324 Adeline F., b. Sept. 10, 1869, m. William Riordan, Feb. 27, 1890.

+325 Florence L., b. June 8, 1871, m. Alfred E. Jackson, Dec. 25, 1890.

326 Frank L., b. June 8, 1871, d. Jan. 3, 1873.

327 John C., b. Dec. 15, 1873.

+328 Robert L., b. July 12, 1876, m. Adelaide L. Parker, Mar. 9, 1898.

+329 Fred F., b. Aug. 16, 1878, m. Maud M. Sanders, Sept. 23, 1903.

115 BENJAMIN B. AND JOSEPHINE (WRIGHT) COURTRIGHT, issue:

330 Ella J., b. Oct. 5, 1871, d. Feb. 23, 1890.

+331 Jessie E., b. Nov. 29, 1872, m. Edward Larson, Nov. 29, 1891.

332 Evangeline, b. Sept. 25, 1874, m. Albert N. Parker, May 5, 1894.

MRS. CAROLINE (COURTRIGHT) ABBOTT
b. 1842

+333 Mabel C., b. Sept. 12, 1876, m. Maitland Hill, June 14, 1906.
+334 Winfred M., b. Oct. 8, 1878, m. Grace V. Wing, Oct. 18, 1906.
 335 Chester A., b. Jan. 12, 1881.
 336 James A., b. Jan. 12, 1881, d. Jan. 13, 1881.
+337 Gaylord M., b. Dec. 27, 1886, m. Nelle M. Boyd, Sept. 5, 1916.
+338 Guy B., b. Dec. 27, 1886, m. Georgia Miller, Dec. 2, 1915.
+339 Charlotte V., b. Mar. 23, 1891, m. Alexander R. Thompson, Sept. 29, 1914.

116 Peter S. and Harriet A. (Courtright) Mackay, issue:

 340 Mary S., b. Sept. 25, 1863, d. Sept. 3, 1864.
+341 Harriet L., b. June 14, 1866, m. Edward J. McMahon, Jan. 10, 1883, m. 2d, John M. Browning, Sept. 14, 1904.
+342 Harry C., b. Oct. 6, 1869, m. Jana Cady, Jan. 1, 1890.
 343 Hugh R., b. Feb. 25, 1879, d. Jan. 29, 1880.

117 Robert Miner and Caroline A. (Courtright) Abbott, issue:

 344 John Howard, b. Feb. 26, 1866, m. Mabel G. Hax, June 2, 1913.
 345 Carrie Helene, b. Nov. 22, 1867, m. Ira R. Tabor, Nov. 22, 1910.
 346 Robert Bruce, b. Aug. 18, 1873, m. Teckla Engburgh, Dec. 29, 1914, m. 2d, Cora A. Engburgh, June 21, 1919.

118 Cornelius C. and Anna (Newton) Courtright, issue:

+347 Herbert N., b. Aug. 1, 1869, m. Adele M. Dyer, Feb., 1893.
+348 Bessie B., b. Jan. 25, 1871, m. Allison G. Wing, Jan. 16, 1901.
 349 Fred C., b. Mar. 12, 1875, d. Oct. 5, 1875.
 350 Clinton H., b. Feb. 5, 1876, d. July 12, 1876.
 351 Lillian B., b. Apr. 27, 1880.

119 Charles O. and Jennie A. (Fairfield) Courtright, issue:

+352 Ernest H., b. Aug. 18, 1876, m. Elizabeth Leinnar, July 25, 1907.
 353 Arthur W., b. Nov. 15, 1879, d. Feb. 4, 1880.
 354 Ethel L., b. Dec. 27, 1880, m. Emery Painter, Dec. 25, 1906.
 355 Elmer, b. Nov. 15, 1884.
+356 Edna, b. Aug. 5, 1890, m. Roy Trimble, Mar. 4, 1917.
 357 Edith, b. Mar. 4, 1903.

120 Chester O. and Ada M. (Haskins) Courtright, issue:

 358 Hazel Vivian, b. Oct. 26, 1881.

121 John Wilson and Mary T. (Cowles) Chamberlin, issue:

 359 Mary C., b. Apr. 28, 1867, d. Oct. 25, 1881.

121 John Wilson and Livonia R. (Buell) Chamberlin, issue:

 360 John W., b. Mar. 25, 1883, d. Apr. 17, 1914, m. Mary E. Speck, May 23, 1912.

123 Carlton O. and Ruth Ann (Courtright) Lee, issue:
361 Myrta Sarah.

124 Horace P. and Mary E. (Pollard) Courtright, issue:
362 Sarah Blanche, b. Nov. 29, 1873.
363 Edith Anna, b. Sept. 23, 1879, m. Newell Van Bergen, Jan. 8, 1908.

125 Joseph A. and Mary Ellen (Courtright) Bigger, issue:
364 Mina C., b. Jan. 20, 1883, m. Frank C. Cluff, Jan. 20, 1909.

126 Milton L. and Emma E. (Ford) Courtright, issue:
365 Frank Burton, b. June 27, 1872.
366 Carrie E., b. Feb. 7, 1874, d. Jan. 6, 1898.

127 John C. and Mary Leonora (Courtright) Van Natta, issue:
367 Lynn C., b. Mar. 14, 1886, m. Margaret Z. Worley, Nov. 19, 1920.

129 Chancy A. and Lizzie (Battin) Courtright, issue:
+368 Eugene H., b. Jan. 31, 1866, m. Florence B. Yale, Sept. 16, 1888.

131 Edward A. and Mary S. (Courtright) Forrester, issue:
+369 Arthur W., b. Aug. 26, 1870, d. Dec. 16, 1919, m. M. Ella Mc Carthy, Feb. 28, 1894.
370 Harry E., b. May 8, 1875, d. Nov. 5, 1876.
+371 Fred W., b. Jan. 17, 1878, m. Ione Land, June 10, 1903.

132 Thomas J. and Eliza A. (Courtright) Megargel, issue:
+372 Rena M., b. June 5, 1874, d. Jan. 16, 1920, m. George E. Bruorton, June 5, 1902.
+373 Willard C., b. Feb. 21, 1877, m. Matilda Westpfahl, June 23, 1897.
374 Archibald H., b. Mar. 23, 1879.
+375 Ethel J., b. Jan. 28, 1881, d. Nov. 30, 1906, m. Alexander P. Clark, Sept. 10, 1903.
376 Helen R., b. June 17, 1885, d. Feb. 22, 1889.

133 George C. and Anna E. (Luce) Courtright, issue:
+377 Edith P., b. Aug. 15, 1879, m. Dr. William B. Powell.
378 Lillian, b. Jan. 1, 1882, d. Jan. 15, 1885.

135 Lorenzo D. and Martha H. (Courtright) Kemmerer, issue:
+379 Edwin W., b. June 29, 1875, m. M. Rachel Dieckle, Dec. 24, 1901.
380 Jessaline, b. June 7, 1877.
381 Harold D., b. Feb. 6, 1880, d. Dec. 21, 1881.

+382   Roy C., b. Apr. 9, 1882, m. Lea Bernardina Anna Lucretia Botzen, Aug. 15, 1911.

+383   Arthur E., b. July 8, 1885, m. Vivian Gleechman, Dec. 12, 1908.

384   Frank L., b. May 21, 1887, m. Alice Lee Wells, Feb. 10, 1916.

137 DORASTUS AND MARTHA R. (LACEY) CONE, issue:

+385   George W., b. Oct. 7, 1859, d. Oct. 26, 1911, m. Cora G. Holmes, Sept. 12, 1882.

386   Catharine E., b. June 16, 1861, d. June 22, 1869.

+387   Raymond J., b. Oct. 28, 1866, m. Sadie (Martz) Mays, Feb. 18, 1901.

+388   Dorastus C., b. June 20, 1868, d. Sept. 20, 1897, m. Blanche M. Setszer, May 17, 1892.

+389   Mary E., b. Jan. 9, 1875, m. James W. Kight, June 27, 1899.

TENTH GENERATION

140 COL. GEORGE AND MARY (COOPER) ROGERS, issue:

390   Nellie, b. Dec. 31, 1867, d. Dec. 30, 1876.

+391   Sarah, b. Dec. 28, 1873, m. Charles B. Hill, Feb. 26, 1895.

141 CHARLES G. AND CARRIE (CADY) COOPER, issue:

392   Henry, b. Nov. 20, 1876, d. July 26, 1894.

141 CHARLES G. AND IRENE (MARTIN) COOPER, issue:

393   Charles, b. Sept. 13, 1902.

142 WELLINGTON E. AND ANNA E. (BROOKS) HURD, issue:

394   Anna E., b. Jan. 8, 1885, m. Earl Savage, June 29, 1911.

143 FRED J. AND LOUIE L. (HURD) REESE, issue

395   Charles W., b. Apr. 5, 1886, m. Iva M. Roosa, Aug. 28, 1918.

396   Frederick D., b. Aug. 5, 1893.

397   Eva L., b. Oct. 5, 1894, d. Nov. 27, 1895.

398   Nellie E., b. July 5, 1896, m. August E. Schwing, May 28, 1921.

144 ADDIS A. AND MARY E. (HURD) CANNON, issue:

+399   Pauline, b. Dec. 30, 1892, m. Herbert H. Aldrich, Apr. 7, 1917.

146 CHARLES J. AND NELLIE (CRANE) HURD, issue:

+400   Nettie E., b. Mar. 22, 1890, m. Harry W. Crafts, Oct. 8, 1909

+401   Carl B., b. July 10, 1893, m. Esther Waldron, June 17, 1916.

402   Anna L., b. Sept. 20, 1901, m. Harry Vaughn, Apr. 28, 1921.

147 JOHN B. AND CHARLOTTE (HEDGES) RUNYAN, issue:

+403   Bentley M., b. July 31, 1872, m. Beulah Hospelhaun, May 25, 1892.

404   Corinne H., b. Nov. 14, 1874.

148 CHARLES C. AND TINA R. (WRIGHT) RUNYAN, issue:

+405   Sadie L., b. Jan. 13, 1875, m. George A. Mead, June 5, 1900.
+406   William B., b. July 10, 1877, m. Ethel M. Ditwiler, June 6, 1911.
407   Charles E., b. May 11, 1890, m. Beatrice L. Gatton, Apr. 16, 1913.

150 MEAD AND IDA (BOYLE) RUNYAN, issue:

408   Frank B., b. Sept. 6, 1875, d. Mar. 17, 1877.
+409   Harry B., b. Jan. 15, 1877, m. Caroline H. Larson, Oct. 5, 1904.

151 UEL R. AND ALMEDA (RUNYAN) PARSONS, issue:

+410   Mary U., b. Aug. 10, 1884, m. James C. McCullough, Sept. 9, 1907.

153 WILLIS M. AND SADIE (MEAD) STURGES, issue:

411   Mary M., b. Apr. 9, 1880.
412   Robert, b. Mar. 20, 1894.

157 JOSEPH MINER AND JOANNA (GOBLE) COURTRIGHT, issue:

413   Rodney H., b. Feb. 26, 1896.
414   Eloise L., b. June 16, 1901.

158 JAMES AND ELIZABETH (COURTRIGHT) WENTZ, issue:

+415   Milton H., b. Oct. 3, 1885, m. Ethyl John, Sept. 23, 1913.
416   Beryl C., b. Nov. 22, 1890.
417   Lieut. Lee B., b. Mar. 3, 1894, m. Verna Bisbing, June 3, 1920.

160 GEORGE B. AND GERTRUDE (COURTRIGHT) WINDSOR, issue:

+418   Hester M., b. Feb. 1, 1893, m. F. M. Forbis, Feb. 29, 1920,
+419   Helen G., b. Oct. 16, 1894, m. Amos H. Begley, July 27, 1916.
420   George Wayne, b. Dec. 12, 1896.
421   Jessie Ruth, b. May 24, 1899.
422   Laura Pearl, b. Apr. 28, 1903.
423   William Deane, b. Aug. 25, 1905.
424   Lillith B., b. Sept. 23, 1907.
425   Geneva E., b. Sept. 21, 1910.
426   Leetha L., b. June 15, 1916.

162 WILLIAM H. AND LILLIAN PEARL (COURTRIGHT) LEE, issue:

427   Evelyn V., b. May 28, 1908.
428   Mabel G., b. Dec. 1, 1909.
429   William H., Jr., b. Nov. 25, 1913.
430   Laura Pearl, b. Nov. 25, 1913.
431   Dorothy Lucile, b. Oct. 21, 1921.

163 MILTON ROY AND MAY (GROTEGUTH) COURTRIGHT, issue:

432   Helen E., b. Dec. 29, 1917, d. Sept. 15, 1920.
433   Roy M., b. Sept. 16, 1919.

164 WILLIAM V. AND ISABELLE (COURTRIGHT) GOOD, issue:

+434 Adda Lorraine, b. June 30, 1889, m. Alonzo L. Marshall, July 5, 1916.

165 DR. GRANVILLE T. AND CLARA (COURTRIGHT) MATLACK, issue:

+435 A. Louise, b. Sept. 25, 1889, m. Joshua L. Miner, June 15, 1919.
436 Frank C., b. July 13, 1891, d. Apr., 1898.
+437 Dorothy T., b. Mar. 4, 1893, m. John C. Haddock, Oct. 5, 1916.
438 Clare C., b. Dec. 22, 1895.

166 JOHN M. AND KATE (DANIELS-STUCKEY) COURTRIGHT, issue:

439 John D., b. June 27, 1911.

168 CHARLES AND JENNIE N. (COURTRIGHT) SHELDON, issue:

440 Anna C., b. Oct. 19, 1897.
441 William A., b. Oct. 11, 1901, m. Evelant M. Baker, Feb. 26, 1921.
442 Benjamin C., b. May 29, 1903, d. June 9, 1908.
443 George M., b. May 3, 1908.
444 Mary H., b. Feb. 11, 1912.

171 WILLIAM W. AND REBA (HENDERSON) COURTRIGHT, issue:

445 Benjamin F., b. Apr. 6, 1907.
446 William W., b. May 3, 1909.
447 Mary R., b. June 19, 1914.

172 JOHN SEARLE AND ELLEN (LATHROP) COURTRIGHT, issue:

448 Sarah L., b. Feb. 10, 1881.
449 Florence, b. Mar. 12, 1892.

173 HARRIE B. AND CLARA IDA (WELLS) COURTRIGHT, issue:

450 Ruth S., b. Jan. 24, 1877, m. David M. Reynolds, Oct. 24, 1906.
+451 Josephine W., b. July 17, 1878, m. William Nathaniel Brooks, Mar. 7, 1906.
452 James Wells, b. Feb. 2, 1887, m. Naomi J. Warner, Dec. 27, 1918.

174 GEORGE R. AND MARY A. (COY) COURTRIGHT, issue:

453 Hugh C., b. Nov. 5, 1893, m. Olive Preen, Aug. 1, 1921.

176 WILBERT W. AND MARY E. (COURTRIGHT) LAMB, issue:

454 Frank C., b. Mar. 17, 1912.

181 HON. HOMER P. AND JESSIE F. (BREESE) SNYDER, issue:

455 Charles Raymond, b. July 13, 1883, d. Oct. 7, 1906.
+456 Estelle Breese, b. Oct. 3, 1885, m. Edward H. Teall, Sept. 14, 1907.
+457 Jessie Florence, b. May 14, 1893, m. Louis E. Thompson, Sept. 10, 1910.

182 JAMES M. AND GRACE (MURRAY) BREESE, issue·

458   William Murray, b. June 9, 1890.
+459 Blanche Frances, b. Nov. 3, 1892, m. Charles A. Sweet, Sept. 27, 1915.
460   Charles Thomas, b. Apr. 18, 1904.

186 JAMES M. AND GERTRUDE (SALENO) COURTRIGHT, issue:

+461 Milton, b. Oct. 5, 1883, m. Sophia Varin, Aug. 2, 1909.
462   Stephen S., b. Dec. 3, 1885, m. Etta Mary Hume, Mar. 7, 1921.

187 JOHN P. AND MARY (McWALTERS) COURTRIGHT, issue:

+463 Florine M., b. Sept. 12, 1880, m. Edward Grabow, Apr. 22, 1901.
464   Alice B., b. Dec. 22, 1882, m. Albert P. Russell, Nov. 28, 1912.
+465 Lillian, b. June 25, 1890, m. John Pringle, June 20, 1914.

188 WILLIAM B. AND LOUISA J. (HAWLEY) COURTRIGHT, issue:

466   Maud B., b. Feb. 18, 1878, d. July 10, 1888.
+467 George B., b. June 29, 1883, m. Margaret W. Robinson, Oct. 11, 1911.
+468 Fidelia B., b. Feb. 16, 1887, m. John Traub, June 19, 1919.
469   Frederick, b. Feb. 16, 1887, d. young.

189 JOHN E. AND LILLIAN FIDELIA (COURTRIGHT) NUGENT, issue:

+470 Louise C., b. Aug. 6, 1881, m. Martin L. Roth, Nov. 1, 1911.
471   Harold A., b. July 1, 1883.

190 JAMES AND DELLIE (BARNUM) VERPLANK, issue:

472   Maud.

191 JOHN WOLFORD AND LOUISE (DOTTERER) MUMPER, issue:

473   William H., b. Jan. 27, 1888, m. Doma Stretch, 1918.
474   Horace W., b. Mar. 4, 1893, m. Eleanor Kinscella, Aug. 26, 1918.

193 JAMES AND MOLLIE (STONE) HANCOCK, issue·

475   Earle C.
476   Elizabeth G.

196 HENRY C. AND SARAH (BUTZ) WHITE, issue:

477   C. Frank, b. June 8, 1865.
478   Laura M., b. June 25, 1868.
479   Grace R., b. June 27, 1875.

197 NORMAN AND SARAH E. (WHITE) TRACY, issue:

480   Ernest.
481   Charles.

198 HARRY S. AND MARGARET B. (WHITE) GILCHRIST, issue:

482   Grace R., b. Feb. 14, 1875, d. Jan. 19, 1901.
+483 J. Fred, b. May 29, 1884, m. Gertrude Scott, Nov. 18, 1908.

202 JOHN S. AND HELEN R. (BARBER) LAZARUS, issue:

+484 Minnie L., b. May 12, 1865, m. Robert B. Richardson, Sept. 11, 1890.

203 JOSEPH B. AND ANNA E. (BENFORD) BARBER, issue:

485 Charles W., b. July 12, 1871, m. Alice Reynolds, June, 1893.
+486 Clyde C., b. Dec. 10, 1876, m. May Price, 1913.
+487 Ethel, b. June 21, 1879, m. Frank Hurd, May 14, 1910.

205 JAMES H. AND MARY MARGARET (BARBER) RUNYON, issue:

488 George W., b. May 10, 1875, m. Maude B. Hay, June 26, 1903.
489 Lena Leota, b. Nov. 18, 1876, m. George R. Tousley, Dec. 16, 1896.

209 WILLIAM T. AND ELIZABETH S. (BARBER) PHILLIPS, issue:

490 Hobart W., b. May 15, 1886.
491 Anacortez, b. Jan. 27, 1890, m. Sidney M. Morris, Nov. 16, 1915.
492 Elizabeth, b. Nov. 29, 1897

210 HENRY H. AND DOVE M. (FOSTER) BARBER, issue:

+493 George W., b. Jan. 5, 1891, m. Nellie K. Lee, Sept. 1, 1913.
494 Gertrude B., b. Nov. 26, 1893, m. Sherrill F. Dewis, Feb. 3, 1915.

215 JUDSON S. AND ROSE C. (WILLIAMS) STARK, issue:

+495 Harry W., b. Dec. 27, 1869, m. Francis M. Sheerer, June 29, 1893.
+496 Clara E., b. Sept. 27, 1871, m. Evan R. Williams, Oct. 17, 1894.

216 JOHN W. AND ELIZABETH (STUDLEY) WILLIAMS, issue:
Asher, Lydia, Gilbert, Henry, Blanche, and Robert.

217 CHESTER B. AND ANNA E. (MARTIN) MOTT, issue:

498 Clarence C., b. July 10, 1894, m. Mary E. Sickler, Nov. 9, 1914.

218 BENAGE S. AND IDA (MOTT) JOSSELYN, issue

499 Dorothy, b. June 12, 1888, m. Archibald McIntyre, Apr. 2, 1911.
500 Mildred, b. July 24, 1891, m. Mason Maughum, Feb. 18, 1914.
+501 Benage S., Jr., b. May 16, 1894, m. Lucille C. Clemons, Nov. 11, 1913.

219 MORRIS A. AND ISADORE (PHILLIPS) McCLENTHEN, issue:

502 Alva B., b. ——, 1877, d. ——, 1881.
+503 Nellie C., b. Aug. 18, 1879, m. John R. Hawkins, Dec. 30, 1911.
504 Harrison J., b. Sept. 29, 1881, m. Florence McKee, June 30, 1920.
505 Lucy A., b. June 14, 1883, m. Charles F. Meltzer, Aug. 28, 1906.
+506 Herman P., b. Aug. 28, 1886, d. Jan. 3, 1909, m. Pearl M. Hamilton, Aug. 28, 1905.
+507 Morris A., b. Aug. 8, 1888, m. Margaret E. O'Brien, Nov. 9, 1909.

+508 Zilpha M., b. Nov. 14, 1890, m. Peter C. Hansen, Jan. 22, 1912.
 509 Isadore M., b. Mar. 28, 1893, m. John D. Wilson, Aug. 6, 1913.
 510 Ruth S., b. June 4, 1896.

221 Herman F. and Ada (Roll) Phillips, issue:

511 Charles F., b. Feb. 22, 1889, d. Oct. 11, 1916.
512 Ruth E., b. June 11, 1891.
513 Margaret C., b. July 21, 1896.
514 Mildred J., b. Jan. 22, 1901.

222 Winfield C. and Bertha (Strong) Phillips, issue:

515 Claude, b. Aug. 30, 1889.

222 Winfield C. and Dora B. (Rivers) Phillips, issue:

+516 Lester K., b. Mar. 15, 1891, m. Rena Wood, Nov. 3, 1912.
 517 Nettie C., b. Dec. 8, 1893, m. Joseph O. Smith.
+518 Marian D., b. Feb. 24, 1894, d. Oct. 27, 1918, m. Frank S. Zeise,
      Aug. 11, 1913.
 519 Millis S., b. Apr. 17, 1900.
 520 Philip G., b. May 19, 1906.

223 Garrick Harding and Ida J. (Rhinefield) Phillips, issue:

521 Harry H., b. Feb. 15, 1893.
522 William, b. Dec. 17, 1896.
+523 Mary Letessia, Apr. 8, 1899, m. Michael Sahyonne, June 15,
      1918.
 524 Albertis, b. Oct. 22, 1906.
 525 Walter, b. Apr. 16, 1910.

229 Burton D. and Lulu C. (Abbott) Herron, issue:

526 Cornelia Courtright, b. Dec. 9, 1903.
527 John Abbott, b. Dec. 29, 1904.
528 Harriet Emeline, b. Oct. 8, 1906, d. Mar. 1, 1907.
529 Helen Johnson, b. Sept. 12, 1910.

232 George and Mayme (Johnson) Wright, issue:

530 Lois, b. Sept. 10, 1908.
531 Bonnie, b. Nov. 3, 1912.

235 Arthur P. and Minnie E. (Wright) Twichell, issue:

532 Mary E., b. Dec. 27, 1893, d. Apr. 2, 1916.
533 Arthur R., b. Apr. 25, 1895.

237 Edward and Jessie E. (Courtright) Larsen, issue:

534 Helen W., b. Mar. 21, 1900.

239 Maitland and Mabel C. (Courtright) Hill, issue:

535 Forrest M., b. Apr. 4, 1909.

536 Winifred C., b. Oct. 24, 1910.
537 Hazel M., b. Dec. 24, 1911.
538 Bernard, b. Sept. 29, 1913.
539 Beatrice, b. Sept. 29, 1913.

240 WINFRED M. AND GRACE V (WING) COURTRIGHT, issue:
540 Robert W., b. Dec. 29, 1909.
541 Janice M., b. June 23, 1914.
542 Joye E., b. Feb. 15, 1915.
543 Donna C., b. Apr. 13, 1918.
544 Edward A., b. Nov. 19, 1921.

242 GAYLORD M. AND NELLE (BOYD) COURTRIGHT, issue:
545 Gaylord B., b. Mar. 11, 1921, d. Mar. 29, 1921.

243 GUY B. AND GEORGIA (MILLER) COURTRIGHT, issue:
546 Jane J., b. Apr. 16, 1917.

244 ALEXANDER R. AND CHARLOTTE V. (COURTRIGHT) THOMP-
       SON, issue:
547 Virginia D., b. Sept. 19, 1916.
548 Mary H., b. Feb. 19, 1921.

246 RICARDO ST. P. AND ANNIE W. (MAUS) LOWRY, issue:
549 George M., b. Oct. 27, 1889, m. Henrietta Brownell, Apr. 14,
       1916, m. 2d, Caroline Coleman, Aug. 17, 1920.
+550 Philip W., b. Nov. 28, 1893, m. Evelyn Holt, June 24, 1916.

247 WALTER C. AND MARGARET C. (GRIFFIN) LOWRY, issue:
+551 Donaldson R., b. Apr. 30, 1892, m. Emily Clark, June 12, 1915.

254 WILLIAM B. AND ALICE E. (LAMB) KELLER, issue:
552 William B., Jr., b. Feb. 11, 1884.

261 CHARLES D. AND ELLEN H. (SNOW) HAWN, issue:
+553 Howard S., b. Apr. 23, 1893, m. Helen Fleming, Mar. 1, 1917.
+554 Orra F., b. June 23, 1896, m. Sarah Powell, June 16, 1920.

262 CHARLES A. AND MAUD J. (SNOW) FOLEY, issue:
555 Ralph J., b. Oct. 15, 1899.
556 Ruth M., b. Sept. 8, 1904.

264 BURTON C. AND ETHEL M. (KELLY) SNOW, issue:
557 Helen E., b. Feb. 8, 1908.

265 FRANK B. AND LILLIAN (COURTRIGHT) THOMPSON, issue:
558 Horatio M., b. Mar. 5, 1885, d. Mar. 2, 1917.
559 Harry C., b. Oct. 13, 1886.

560 A. Howard, b. May 8, 1889, m. Ruth Dennington, June 30, 1913.
561 Helen M., b. Mar. 13, 1895.
562 Rosemond L., b. Mar. 2, 1897, m. William Ryan, June 29, 1917.
563 Willard F., b. Aug. 6, 1899.
564 Russell S., b. Dec. 17, 1902.
565 Theodore R., b. Nov. 6, 1904.
566 Josephine E., b. Dec. 7, 1908, d. Dec. 26, 1912.

266 BENJAMIN AND CHARITY M. (SMITH) COURTRIGHT, issue:

567 John Henry, b. Nov. 5, 1896, d. Nov. 20, 1896.
+568 Julia Leona, b. Feb. 15, 1898, m. Stephen Dymond, Nov. 14, 1914.
569 Charles Wesley, b. July 7, 1899.
570 Edward Leslie, b. July 13, 1906, d. July 18, 1906.

269 OLIVER R. AND HARRIET (COURTRIGHT) MOORE, issue:

571 Paul R., b. Sept. 22, 1891, m. Emily Morgan, Aug. 28, 1917.
572 Lena A., b. July 28, 1893, m. William S. Armstrong, June 10, 1918.
+573 Ernest H., b. Mar. 14, 1895, m. Coraleta Arnold, Feb. 15, 1918.
+574 Raymond R., b. Oct. 28, 1897, m. Clara B. Steele, Apr. 26, 1919.
+575 Nancy G., b. July 2, 1902, m. Charles M. Slinker, June 30, 1919.
576 Oliver R., b. Mar. 1, 1905, d. Sept. 10, 1911.
577 Dorothy H., b. Aug. 14, 1906, d. Mar. 11, 1907.
578 Edward T., b. Aug. 20, 1910, d. Sept. 10, 1910.
579 Harriet A., b. July 27, 1913.

271 EDWARD T. AND ELIZABETH (COURTRIGHT) EVANS, issue:

580 Richard H., b. Jan. 2, 1902.
581 Harriet Virginia, b. Feb. 2, 1903.
582 Marian L., b. Jan. 9, 1907, d. May 3, 1910.

278 OSCAR C. AND LAURA (BAILEY) LEWIS, issue:

+583 Laura, b. Nov. 26, 1892, m. Harry Krebaum, Nov. 26, 1914.
584 Musa, b. June 23, 1898.

279 WALTER A. AND FRANCES E. (LEWIS) LEWIS, issue:

+585 Ernest B., b. Jan. 19, 1890, m. Maud R. Swan, Dec. 24, 1910.
+586 Everett A., b. Jan. 23, 1894, m. Ada J. Jackson, Oct. 4, 1916.
+587 W. Claire, b. June 30, 1895, m. Henrietta C. Usher, Nov. 6, 1915.
+588 B. Marie, b. May 17, 1897, m. Fred J. Bassett, Mar. 4, 1918.
589 A. Rexford, b. July 26, 1899.

280 EVERETT B. AND ESTELLE (FLAGLER) LEWIS, issue:

590 Harold F., b. Feb. 17, 1895.
591 Kathryn L., b. Jan. 31, 1910.

281 CORNELIUS W. AND ALICE (LEWIS) HOOGHOUSE, issue:

592 Frederick L., b. June 28, 1895, d. July 15, 1902.
+593 Jennie C., b. July 28, 1898, m. Frank A. Dickey, Mar. 30, 1918.

594 C. Beaumont, b. Jan. 27, 1904.
595 Lewis E., b. Dec. 1, 1909.
596 Benjamin E., b. Aug. 20, 1912.

282 LEROY AND BLANCHE (LEWIS) STINES, issue:
597 Richard L., b. Feb. 21, 1912.
598 Margaret E., b. June 11, 1916.

284 LESTER AND LAURA A. (COURTRIGHT) HOUGH, issue:
599 Marion C., b. July 19, 1898.

290 ARCHIE B. AND BERTHA (MORGAN) COURTRIGHT, issue:
600 Harriet Elizabeth, b. Aug. 23, 1917.

292 ALBERT W. AND NINA M. (COURTRIGHT) GABRIEL, issue:
601 Doris Alberta, b. June 18, 1914.
602 Albert Washburn, b. June 29, 1916.

293 SAMUEL H. AND MARY E. (PRATT) STEVENS, issue:
+603 Charles B., b. Mar. 21, 1875, m. Harriet Berry, Nov. 5, 1902.
+604 Helen L., b. Jan. 8, 1878, m. Charles W. Hurlbut, Sept. 5, 1901, m. 2d, Duncan T. Campbell, Oct. 6, 1919.
605 Walter P., b. Mar. 13, 1882, m. Anna McAnulty, Apr. 11, 1912.

294 WILLIAM B. AND LOUISE B. (PRATT) HENWOOD, issue:
606 Richard P., b. July 30, 1878, d. July 8, 1899.
+607 Catherine L., b. Nov. 17, 1880, m. Turvey Breese, June 27, 1906.

295 JAMES L. AND LEONORA (PRATT) CONNELL, issue:
+608 Lawrence M., b. Apr. 27, 1885, m. Cynthia Magee, July 8, 1914.
+609 Carleton A., b. Apr. 23, 1888, m. Lydia Taggart, Sept. 25, 1920.
610 Mary L., b. Sept. 18, 1893.

296 CLAUDIUS B. AND HELEN (WAGNER) PRATT, issue:
611 Helen M., b. Aug. 4, 1893, d. Nov. 26, 1897.
+612 Geraldine Marie, b. Dec. 29, 1894, m. Herbert Lewis Handy, Apr. 15, 1914.
613 Harold S., b. Nov. 28, 1896.

297 JAMES P. AND MARY ALICE (PHELPS) CROSSLEY, issue:
614 John P., b. Aug. 26, 1875, m. Mayme I. Hogue, June 24, 1908.
615 Bertha J., b. Apr. 1, 1879.
+616 J. Le Grand A., b. Jan. 2, 1882, m. Gail H. Hardesty, Sept. 14, 1904.
617 Ruby Geraldine, b. Oct. 5, 1884.
+618 Clinton C., b. Mar. 4, 1887, m. Sara B. Rees, June 12, 1913.

298 HORACE G. AND MARY A. (O'SHEA) PHELPS, issue:
619 William J., b. Jan. 21, 1886.
+620 Cassie E., b. Sept. 22, 1887, m. Harry G. McCleary, June 24, 1908.

299 FRANK J. AND FLOY H. (PHELPS) DIGNON, issue:

+621 Sidney Le Grand, b. Oct. 17, 1890, m. Cecelia A. Wheeler, June 8, 1916.

300 ALBERT B. AND JANNIE C. (PHELPS) CORCILIUS, issue:

622 Phyllis Lenore, b. Mar. 2, 1893.

305 CARSON E. AND MINNIE L. (BENNETT) PHILLIPS, issue:

+623 Edith B., b. Apr. 9, 1887, m. Ferdinand Ferbrache, July 23, 1908.

307 LESLIE S. AND SADIE A. (DAVISON) PHILLIPS, issue:

624 Howard L., b. Mar. 15, 1879, m. Mae Bell Collins, Sept. 3, 1907.

310 J. CHANNING AND MINNIE J. (PHILLIPS) SEATON, issue:

+625 Nina R., b. Nov. 5, 1885, m. Charles E. Smith, Feb. 16, 1907.

311 ALFRED E. AND MARY LOUISE (PHILLIPS) HARDING, issue:

+626 Alfred Leslie, b. Mar. 21, 1888, m. Georgia N. Watkins, Apr. 27, 1907, m. 2d, Mae London, Aug. 14, 1915.

314 CHARLES SIGEL AND ANNA M. (SCHLAMPP) COURTRIGHT, issue:

+627 Ouida B., b. July 21, 1888, m. James E. Herweg, June 21, 1916.
+628 Charles S., Jr., b. Mar. 25, 1890, m. Marion H. Gilbert, Sept. 29, 1917.

315 ALBERT W. AND LILLIAN N. (COURTRIGHT) ARNOLD, issue:

+629 Nina, b. Nov. 30, 1888, m. Oliver P. Goodspeed, Sept. 27, 1911.

316 ELMER F. AND MYRTLE R. (COURTRIGHT) CODDINGTON, issue:

+630 Hazel R., b. Aug. 30, 1886, m. Nelson A. Sanford, Oct. 23, 1909.

319 ALONZO E. AND CLARA V. (WUNDER) COURTRIGHT, issue:

631 Horace E., b. May 7, 1884.
+632 Clara V., b. May 18, 1889, m. Wayne W. O'Neal, Jan. 29, 1911.
+633 William A., b. Feb. 28, 1895, m. Merle Vail, Sept. 24, 1919.

320 HARRY M. AND MOLLIE G. (SHAFTER) COURTRIGHT, issue:

634 Harry C., b. June 18, 1889, m. Elizabeth G. Hathaway, Aug. 25, 1913.

321 OSCAR W. AND HATTIE L. (RUBLE) BROWN, issue:

635 Charles E., b. Dec. 28, 1880, d. June 3, 1894.
+636 Harvey F., b. Dec. 9, 1888, d. Dec. 12, 1918, m. Grace E. Hopkins, May 19, 1909.

322 LOUIS AND CARRIE L. (RUBLE) WEEKS, issue:

+637 Harry V., b. Mar. 16, 1888, m. Laura L. Logan, June 18, 1910.

324 WILLIAM AND ADELINE F. (RUBLE) RIORDAN, issue:
+638 Blanche, b. July 27, 1891, m. George Sleezer, Feb. 11, 1915.

325 ALFRED E. AND FLORENCE L. (RUBLE) JACKSON, issue:
639 Howard L., b. Jan. 4, 1892, d. May 31, 1903.
640 Dale V., b. Mar. 6, 1893, d. Apr. 13, 1894.
641 Florence M., b. May 2, 1897, d. Oct. 16, 1918.
642 Ruby R., b. Nov. 15, 1899.
643 Mildred L., b. May 2, 1902.
644 Edith A., b. May 25, 1904.
645 Alfred R., b. Apr. 5, 1906.
646 Grace L., b. Oct. 31, 1909.

328 ROBERT L. AND ADELAIDE L. (PARKER) RUBLE, issue:
647 Robert A., b. Aug. 29, 1899, m. Hallie Pence, Sept. 15, 1921.
648 Dorothy E., b. Mar. 25, 1903.
649 John L., b. June 25, 1914.

329 FRED F. AND MAUD M. (SANDERS) RUBLE, issue:
650 Claude R., b. June 13, 1905.
651 John E., b. May 26, 1910, d. June 1, 1910.
652 Beulah G., b. Sept. 9, 1911.
653 Francis M., b. July 15, 1913.
654 Morris L., b. June 30, 1916.

331 EDWARD AND JESSIE E. (COURTRIGHT) LARSEN, issue:
655 Helen W., b. Mar. 21, 1900.

333 MAITLAND AND MABEL C. (COURTRIGHT) HILL, issue:
656 Forrest M., b. Apr. 4, 1909.
657 Winifred C., b. Oct. 24, 1910.
658 Hazel M., b. Dec. 24, 1911.
659 Bernard, b. Sept. 29, 1913.
660 Beatrice, b. Sept. 29, 1913.

334 WINFRED M. AND GRACE V (WING) COURTRIGHT, issue:
661 Robert W., b. Dec. 29, 1909.
662 Janice M., b. June 23, 1914.
663 Joye E., b. Feb. 15, 1915.
664 Donna C., b. Apr. 13, 1918.
665 Edward A., b. Nov. 19, 1921.

337 GAYLORD M. AND NELLE M. (BOYD) COURTRIGHT, issue:
666 Gaylord B., b. Mar. 11, 1921, d. Mar. 29, 1921.

338 GUY B. AND GEORGIA (MILLER) COURTRIGHT, issue:
667 Jane J., b. Apr. 16, 1919.

339 Alexander R. and Charlotte V. (Courtright) Thompson, issue:
668 Virginia D., b. Sept. 19, 1916.
669 Mary Helen, b. Feb. 19, 1921.

341 Edward J. and Harriet L. (Mackay) McMahon, issue:
670 Helen S., b. Sept. 1, 1884, d. Oct. 31, 1908, m. John Douglas, Oct. 14, 1906.

342 Harry C. and Jana (Cady) Mackay, issue·
671 Raymond C., b. Oct. 17, 1891.
672 Ralph S., b. Apr. 12, 1898, m. Helen N. Severance, May 24, 1922.

347 Herbert N. and Adele M. (Dyer) Courtright, issue:
673 Gerald D., b. Dec. 10, 1893.
674 Helen A., b. Mar. 10, 1897, d. Oct. 26, 1907.
675 Cornelius H., b. Jan. 27, 1911.
676 Volentine, b. Aug. 17, 1913.

348 Allison G. and Bessie B. (Courtright) Wing, issue:
677 Wendell C., b. Apr. 14, 1906.

352 Ernest H. and Elizabeth (Leinnar) Courtright, issue:
678 Eleanor V., b. Mar. 21, 1918.

356 Roy and Edna (Courtright) Trimble, issue:
679 Paul L., b. Oct. 24, 1920.

368 Eugene H. and Florence B. (Yale) Courtright, issue:
680 Laura E., b. Jan. 7, 1890.

369 Arthur W. and M. Ella (McCarthy) Forrester, issue:
681 Luella M., b. June 20, 1895.
682 Edward B., b. Sept. 27, 1898, d. June 27, 1917.

371 Fred W. and Ione (Land) Forrester, issue:
683 Ione, b. Aug. 23, 1906.
684 Fred W., b. Sept. 25, 1909.

372 George E. and Rena M. (Megargel) Bruorton, issue:
685 Rena Eliza, b. May 5, 1903.
686 George E., b. Nov. 5, 1906, d. Mar. 4, 1907.
687 Ethel Josephine, Jan. 13, 1908.
688 Winifred Louise, Apr. 5, 1915.

373 Willard C. and Matilda (Westpfahl) Megargel, issue:
689 Harold J., b. Feb. 1, 1899.
690 Charles E., b. June 15, 1904.

375 ALEXANDER P. AND ETHEL J. (MEGARGEL) CLARK, issue:
691 Alexander P., b. Aug. 6, 1905.
692 Ethelbert E., b. Nov. 27, 1906, d. Feb. 1, 1907.

377 DR. WILLIAM B. AND EDITH P. (COURTRIGHT) POWELL,
issue
693 Richard Frederick.

379 EDWIN W. AND M. RACHEL (DIECKLE) KEMMERER, issue:
694 Donald L., b. Dec. 24, 1905.
695 Ruth, b. Nov. 6, 1909.

382 ROY C. AND LEA (BOTZEN) KEMMERER, issue:
696 Lorenzo B., b. Apr. 25, 1914.
697 Ethel L., b. Oct. 7, 1915.
698 Doris E., b. July 22, 1921.

383 ARTHUR E. AND VIVIAN (GLEECHMAN) KEMMERER, issue:
699 Dorothy L, b. Jan. 24, 1911.
700 Martha J., b. Dec. 16, 1916.

385 GEORGE W. AND CORA G. (HOLMES) CONE, issue:
+701 Helen H., b. Aug. 5, 1883, d. Sept. 16, 1909, m. Logan E. Old,
Apr. 19, 1905.
+702 Pauline L., b. Dec. 29, 1885, m. Rev. Oscar E. Sams, May 8, 1906.
+703 George S., b. Feb. 27, 1889, m. Elva Odessa Ludwig, Jan. 29,
1913.
704 Mildred C., b. June 14, 1895.

387 RAYMOND J. AND SADIE (MARTZ-MAYS) CONE, issue:
705 Dorastus L., b. Sept. 6, 1902.
706 Raymond L., b. July 12, 1909.
707 George W., b. Aug. 6, 1912.

388 DORASTUS C. AND BLANCHE (SETSZER) CONE, issue:
708 Alfred D., b. June 6, 1893, m. Janet Waugh, June 1, 1918.
+709 Henry S., b. Nov. 30, 1894, m. Mary Anna Palmer, Apr. 8, 1917.

389 JAMES W. AND MARY E. (CONE) KIGHT, issue:
710 Martha A., b. Dec. 23, 1900.
711 James W., b. Apr. 3, 1908.

ELEVENTH GENERATION

391 CHARLES B. AND SARAH (ROGERS) HILL, issue:
712 Isabelle, b. Aug. 27, 1899.
713 Charles B., b. Nov. 30, 1901.
714 Helen, b. Jan. 14, 1903.

399 HERBERT H. AND PAULINE (CANNON) ALDRICH, issue:
715   Mason H., b. Apr. 27, 1919.
716   Herbert C., b. Aug. 7, 1920.

400 HARRY W. AND NETTIE (HURD) CRAFTS, issue:
717   Norma, b. Nov. 8, 1910.

401 CARL B. AND ESTHER (WALDRON) HURD, issue:
718   Carl B., Jr., b. Sept. 20, 1919.

403 BENTLEY M. AND BEULAH (HOSPELHAUN) RUNYAN, issue:
719   John B., b. Mar. 17, 1894, d. Dec. 5, 1899.
720   George H., b. June 24, 1896.

405 GEORGE A. AND SADIE (RUNYAN) MEAD, issue:
721   Mary W., b. May 10, 1911.

406 WILLIAM B. AND ETHEL (DITWILER) RUNYAN, issue:
722   John D., b. Apr. 8, 1912.
723   William B., Jr., b. June 26, 1918.

409 HARRY B. AND CAROLINE H. (LARSON) RUNYAN, issue:
724   Robert M., b. Nov. 15, 1905.
725   Evelyn R., b. Jan. 11, 1910.

410 JAMES C. AND MARY U. (RUNYAN) McCULLOUGH, issue:
726   Katharine C., b. Mar. 2, 1911.
727   Uel P., b. Nov. 20, 1913.

415 MILTON H. AND ETHYL (JOHN) WENTZ, issue:
728   John Milton, b. July 9, 1914.

418 F. M. AND HESTER M. (WINDSOR) FORBIS, issue:
729   Hubert L., b. May 1, 1921.

419 AMOS H. AND HELEN G. (WINDSOR) BEGLEY, issue:
730   Ruth G., b. June 26, 1918.
731   Etta M., b. Oct. 31, 1919.
732   Margaret L., b. Apr. 29, 1921.

434 ALONZO L. AND ADDA LORRAINE (GOOD) MARSHALL, issue:
733   Gertrude I., b. Nov. 27, 1918.
734   Val. A., b. May 8, 1921.
735   Helen L., b. May 8, 1921.

435 JOSHUA L. AND A. LOUISE (MATLACK) MINER, issue:
736   Joshua L., 3d, b. July 11, 1920.

437 JOHN C. AND DOROTHY T. (MATLACK) HADDOCK, issue:
737   Clare M., b. Aug. 30, 1917.

451 WILLIAM N. AND JOSEPHINE W. (COURTRIGHT) BROOKS, issue:

738 Nathaniel C., b. Jan. 9, 1908.
739 Claruth, b. Apr. 3, 1909.

456 EDWARD H. AND ESTELLE B. (SNYDER) TEALL, issue:

740 Homer S., b. Nov. 8, 1908.
741 Sarah H., b. Dec. 27, 1909.
742 Jessie B., b. Dec. 5, 1911.

457 LOUIS E. AND JESSIE F. (SNYDER) THOMPSON, issue:

743 Edwin S., b. July 27, 1911, d. Feb. 15, 1914.
744 Thomas W., b. Oct. 20, 1913.

459 CHARLES A. AND BLANCHE F. (BREESE) SWEET, issue:

745 Murray B., b. June 7, 1917.
746 Paul H., b. Jan. 27, 1919.

461 MILTON AND SOPHIA (VARIN) COURTRIGHT, issue:

747 Celina M., b. Nov. 22, 1910.
748 James M., b. Dec. 16, 1914.
749 George V., b. June 24, 1916.
750 Joseph W., b. Mar. 18, 1918.
751 Homer C., b. Apr. 19, 1921.

463 EDWARD AND FLORINE M. (COURTRIGHT) GRABOW, issue:

752 Jean C., b. Apr. 22, 1904.
753 Mary C., b. Apr. 27, 1907.

465 JOHN AND LILLIAN (COURTRIGHT) PRINGLE, issue:

754 John C., b. Dec. 12, 1914.
755 Amy Neal, b. Mar. 12, 1918.

467 GEORGE B. AND MARGARET W. (ROBINSON) COURTRIGHT, issue:

756 Marian Jane, b. Oct. 31, 1912.
757 Fidelia E., b. Mar. 14, 1917.

468 JOHN AND FIDELIA B. (COURTRIGHT) TRAUB, issue:

758 Florence A., b. Apr. 13, 1920.

470 MARTIN L. AND LOUISE C. (NUGENT) ROTH, issue:

759 Marian L., b. Sept. 6, 1912.
760 Martin L., Jr., b. June 11, 1914.

483 J. FRED AND GERTRUDE (SCOTT) GILCHRIST, issue:

761 Thomas R., b. Sept. 10, 1909.
762 Glenn E., b. June 21, 1911, d. Dec. 19, 1918.
763 Ileen Isabel, b. Mar. 25, 1921.

484 ROBERT B. AND MINNIE L. (LAZARUS) RICHARDSON, issue:

+764 John C., b. May 11, 1892, m. Helen C. Gill, Sept. 29, 1917, m. 2d, Irene Reisenberg, Oct. 15, 1921.

486 CLYDE C. AND MAY (PRICE) BARBER, issue,

765 Marian Ida, b. Feb. 26, 1915.

487 FRANK AND ETHEL (BARBER) HURD, issue:

766 Margaret L., b. Feb. 5, 1918.

493 GEORGE W. AND NELLIE K. (LEE) BARBER, issue:

767 Pauline D., b. Feb. 25, 1914.
768 Elizabeth R., b. Feb. 10, 1916.
769 Harrison L., b. Mar. 27, 1918.
770 Thomas M. b. May 10, 1921.

495 HARRY W. AND FRANCES M. (SHEARER) STARK, issue:

771 Ethel, b. Feb. 2, 1894, d. Sept. 25, 1903.
772 Marian L., b. Sept. 9, 1895.
773 Frances, b. July 17, 1897, d. July 4, 1913.
+774 Helen A., b. June 20, 1899, m. Ralph Bunnel, Nov. 18, 1920.
775 Ruth, b. Jan. 30, 1901.
776 Mildred, b. Oct. 10, 1904.
777 Harry, b. Aug 16, 1906.
778 Marjory, b. Oct. 9, 1908.

496 EVAN R. AND CLARA E. (STARK) WILLIAMS, issue:

779 Bernice S., b. July 15, 1895.
+780 Harry E., b. May 11, 1897, m. May Trethaway, Nov. 25, 1919.
781 Margaret L., b. Sept. 18, 1899.
782 Gladys I., b. Nov. 22, 1901.
+783 Rose C., b. Apr. 28, 1903, m. Donald Heddon, May 28, 1921.
784 Sheldon R., b. Sept. 4, 1904.
785 Jean M., b. Sept. 7, 1906.
786 Milton, b. Apr. 27, 1908, d. May 3, 1908.
787 Paul S., b. Feb. 2, 1914.
788 Elizabeth C., b. Apr. 4, 1915.

501 BENAGE S., JR., AND LUCILLE (CLEMONS) JOSSELYN, issue:

789 Gail Clemons, b. June 11, 1916.

503 JOHN R. AND NELLIE C. (McCLENTHEN) HAWKINS, issue:

790 Marjorie June, b. June 12, 1913.
791 Eleanor Marie, b. Oct. 10, 1915.

506 HERMAN P. AND PEARL M. (HAMILTON) McCLENTHEN, issue:

792 Herman P., b. July 10, 1907.

507 MORRIS A. AND MARGARET E. (O'BRIEN) McCLENTHEN,
issue:
793 Harrison C., b. June 4, 1910.
794 Margaret F., b. Apr. 18, 1912.

508 PETER C. AND ZILPHA M. (McCLENTHEN) HANSON, issue:
795 Walter W., b. Nov. 20, 1912.
796 Homèr C., b. Nov. 29, 1913.

516 LESTER K. AND RENA (WOOD) PHILLIPS, issue:
797 Ruth I., b. Oct. 20, 1913.
798 Esther M., b. Dec. 17, 1916.

518 FRANK S. AND MARIAN D. (PHILLIPS) ZEISE, issue:
799 William E., b. Feb. 20, 1914, d. Nov. 13, 1919.
800 Frank S., Jr., b. Nov. 30, 1916.

523 MICHAEL AND MARY LETESSIA (PHILLIPS) SAHYONNE,
issue:
801 Mary, b. Nov. 11, 1919.

550 PHILIP W. AND EVELYN (HOLT) LOWRY, issue:
802 Philip H., b. Feb. 20, 1918.
803 Marion, b. Apr. 15, 1921.

551 DONALDSON R. AND EMILY (CLARK) LOWRY, issue:
804 Charlotte C., b. Nov. 4, 1918.
805 Donaldson R., b. Oct. 24, 1920.

553 HOWARD S. AND HELEN (FLEMING) HAWN, issue:
806 Ellen V., b. Nov. 10, 1921.

554 ORRA F. AND SARAH (POWELL) HAWN, issue:
807 Elizabeth B., b. June 25, 1921.

568 STEPHEN AND JULIA (COURTRIGHT) DYMOND, issue:
808 Lena Elmira, b. May 3, 1915.
809 John Henry, b. May 17, 1916.
810 Hazel Alberta, b. June 26, 1918.

573 ERNEST H. AND CORALETA (ARNOLD) MOORE, issue:
811 Virginia L., b. Mar. 10, 1921.

574 RAYMOND R. AND CLARA (STEELE) MOORE, issue:
812 Clara B., b. Sept. 12, 1920.

575 CHARLES M. AND NANCY G. (MOORE) SLINKER, issue:
813 Charles S., b. Mar. 1, 1920, d. Mar. 23, 1920.
814 Marian E., b. June 10, 1921.

583 HARRY W. AND LAURA (LEWIS) KREBAUM, issue:
815 Don W., b. Feb. 9, 1918.

585 ERNEST B. AND MAUD R. (SWAN) LEWIS, issue:
816 Ruth M., b. Dec. 14, 1912.
817 Walter R., b. June 7, 1916.

586 EVERETT A. AND ADA J. (JACKSON) LEWIS, issue:
818 Jean V., b. May 15, 1921.

587 W. CLAIRE AND HENRIETTA C. (USHER) LEWIS, issue:
819 Doris M., b. Feb. 17, 1917.
820 Walter G., b. Oct. 3, 1918.
821 Ralph C., b. Jan. 27, 1920.

588 FRED J. AND B. MARIE (LEWIS) BASSETT, issue:
822 Dorothy G., b. Jan. 30, 1920.
823 Donna M., b. June 30, 1921.

593 FRANK A. AND JENNIE C. (HOOGHOUSE) DICKEY, issue:
824 Earl A., b. Sept. 12, 1918.
825 Cornelius R., b. Sept. 21, 1920.

603 CHARLES B. AND HARRIET (BERRY) STEVENS, issue:
826 Helen M., b. Mar. 15, 1904.

604 CHARLES W. AND HELEN L. (STEVENS) HURLBUT, issue:
827 John S., b. Mar. 8, 1904.
828 Charles W., Jr., b. Mar. 17, 1907.

607 TURVEY AND CATHERINE L. (HENWOOD) BREESE, issue:
829 Richard H., b. Jan. 17, 1910.
830 John T., b. July 3, 1912.

608 LAWRENCE M. AND CYNTHIA (MAGEE) CONNELL, issue:
831 Lawrence M., Jr., b. June 15, 1916.
832 Mary L., b. Sept. 16, 1918.

609 CARLETON A. AND LYDIA (TAGGART) CONNELL, issue:
833 Carleton A., Jr., b. Oct. 23, 1921.

612 HERBERT L. AND GERALDINE M. (PRATT) HANDY, issue:
834 Jane, b. June 26, 1915.
835 Gretchen, b. Aug. 22, 1917.
836 Herbert L., 3d, b. June 15, 1919.

616 J. LE GRAND AND GAIL H. (HARDESTY) CROSSLEY, issue:
837 Virginia G., b. Aug. 3, 1905.

838 John D., b. July 4, 1908.
839 Robert L., b. Dec. 23, 1909.

618 CLINTON C. AND SARA B. (REES) CROSSLEY, issue:
840 Rees D., b. May 24, 1920.

620 HARRY G. AND CASSIE E. (PHELPS) MCCLEARY, issue:
841 Robert G., b. Mar. 9, 1910, d. Mar. 20, 1910.
842 Margaret M., b. Feb. 10, 1913.

621 SIDNEY L. AND CECELIA A. (WHEELER) DIGNON, issue:
843 Francis H., b. Jan. 18, 1920.

623 FERDINAND AND EDITH B. (PHILLIPS) FERBRACHE, issue:
844 Gerald P., b. Sept. 26, 1909.
845 Mildred M., b. July 4, 1916.

625 CHARLES E. AND NINA R. (SEATON) SMITH, issue:
846 Minnie P., b. July 16, 1911.
847 Donald C., b. Feb. 11, 1915.

626 ALFRED L. AND GEORGIA N. (WATKINS) HARDING, issue:
848 C. Louise, b. Dec. 3, 1908.

627 JAMES E. AND OUIDA B. (COURTRIGHT) HERWEG, issue:
849 Marjorie L., b. June 23, 1919.

628 CHARLES S., JR., AND MARION H. (GILBERT) COURTRIGHT,
        issue ·
850 Lydia Ann, b. July 25, 1918.

629 OLIVER P. AND NINA (ARNOLD) GOODSPEED, issue:
851 David Courtright, b. Sept. 21, 1916.

630 NELSON A. AND HAZEL R. (CODDINGTON) SANFORD, issue:
852 Catherine E., b. Aug. 16, 1913.
853 Elizabeth M., b. Dec. 18, 1915.

632 WAYNE W. AND CLARA V (COURTRIGHT) O'NEAL, issue:
854 Wayne W., b. Nov. 27, 1911.
855 Clara V., b. Oct. 11, 1913.

633 WILLIAM A. AND MERLE (VAIL) COURTRIGHT, issue:
856 Wilma J., b. Sept. 3, 1920.

636 HARVEY F. AND GRACE E. (HOPKINS) BROWN, issue:
857 William H., b. Apr. 28, 1912.

637 HARRY V. AND LAURA L. (LOGAN) WEEKS, issue:
858 John L., b. Dec. 11, 1916.
859 Helen B., b. Dec. 11, 1920.

638 GEORGE AND BLANCHE (RIORDAN) SLEEZER, issue:
860 Lorna M., b. Oct 11, 1916.
861 Shirley V., b. Mar. 27, 1918.

701 LOGAN E. AND HELEN H. (CONE) OLD, issue:
862 Logan E., Jr., b. Feb. 2, 1906.
863 George Y., b. July 21, 1909, d. Sept. 18, 1909

702 REV. OSCAR E. AND PAULINE L. (CONE) SAMS, issue:
864 Oscar E., Jr., b. Dec. 18, 1907.
865 Conway C., b. Dec. 8, 1914.

703 GEORGE S. AND ELVA ODESSA (LUDWIG) CONE, issue:
866 Phoebe L., b. Nov. 12, 1913.
867 George S., Jr., b. July 7, 1915.
868 Helen H., b. Sept. 26, 1917.

709 HENRY S. AND MARY A. (PALMER) CONE, issue:
869 Nellie Monroe, b. July 2, 1918.
870 Maryanne, b. Aug. 1, 1920.

TWELFTH GENERATION

764 JOHN AND HELEN C. (GILL) RICHARDSON issue:
871 Mary Helen, b. July 25, 1918.

774 RALPH AND HELEN A. (STARK) BUNNEL, issue:
872 Jean Marie, b. Sept. 25, 1921.

780 HARRY E. AND MAY (TRETHAWAY) WILLIAMS, issue:
873 Marion Elizabeth, b. Aug. 13, 1921.

783 DONALD AND ROSE (WILLIAMS) HEDDON, issue:
874 Donald Jack, b. Dec. 10, 1921.

DESCENDANTS OF JOHANNES CORTRIGHT

(See pages 39 and 50)

JOHANNES CORTRIGHT, son of Cornelis Hendricksen and Christina (Roosekrans) Cortright, was born at Marbletown, Ulster County, N. Y., bap. at Kingston, Aug. 15, 1714, and m. Margriet Dennemarken, Jan. 24, 1735. He removed to the Minisink, first settling in the "lower neighborhood" of this district, located in Sussex County, N. J., where in 1731 Johannes Westbrook deeded to him and others, a tract of land for a burying ground and school, the first record of him there.

His brother, Hendrick, also lived there at the time, and both were pioneer settlers in this new country, with other Hollanders who emigrated from Kingston, Marbletown, Hurley, Rochester and other places in Ulster County early in the eighteenth century.

With his family, he removed to Northampton County (now Monroe), Pa. about 1744, across the Delaware River, where he purchased a farm, located in Lower Smithfield Township, his future home.

In 1772, he was assessed there a proprietary tax of four pounds, his son John, Jr., twelve shillings, Christopher, one pound, six shillings and eight pence, and Elisha the same amount.

Johannes and Margaret (Dennemarken) Courtright had issue:

John, bap. Nov. 1, 1738, m. Maria Van Vliet.
Christopher, bap. June 17, 1740, m. Martha Miller.
Samuel, bap. July 5, 1742.
+Elisha, bap. Jan. 13, 1745, m. Alida (or Huldah) Dingman.
Abraham Van Kampen, bap. Oct. 2, 1748, m. Effie Drake.
Elizabeth, bap. Sept. 3, 1751, m. John Schoonover.
Christina, bap. June 9, 1754.

ELISHA CORTRIGHT, m. Alida (or Huldah) Dingman prior to 1768, removed to the Wyoming Valley about 1774, first settling at Hanover, but later went to Salem, Luzerne County, where he was a farmer.

He survived the battle of Wyoming, July 3, 1778, but his brothers John and Christopher were both killed, their names inscribed on the monument at Wyoming with the other patriots who were killed. Elisha d. in 1821, was buried in Beach Grove Cemetery, having had:

Cornelia, b. Oct. 20, 1768, m. Emanuel Hoover.
+Abraham, b. 1769, m. Sarah Bouchter.
Eva, b. Mar. 4, 1774, m. Aaron Writer.
+Isaac, b. 1776, m. Mary Dodson.
+Andrew, b. 1780, m. Matilda Bowman.

Margaret, m. James Santee.
Ellen, m. Joseph Rhodes.

ABRAM AND SARAH (BOUCHTER) CORTRIGHT, issue:
+Elisha, b. 1795, m. Sarah Klinetop.
+John B., b. 1796, m. Nancy Santee, m. 2d, Eliza Pollock.
Margaret, b. 1800, m. Solomon Parker.
Ellen, b. 1806, m. Martin Line, m. 2d, Gerard Harrison.
+Isaac, b. 1808, m. Mary Pollock.
+Joseph, b. 1810, m. Lydia Klinetop.

ISAAC AND MARY (DODSON) CORTRIGHT, issue:
+Elisha, b. 1803, m. Martha Cole.
Mabel, b. 1805, m. John Ramsay.
Nancy, b. 1808, m. Barton Mott.
Thomas D., b. 1810, m. Lydia Bidlack.
Huldah, b: 1813.
+Nathan D., b. 1815, m. Margaretta L. Harlan, Feb. 6, 1845.
+Abraham, b. 1817, m. Elizabeth Lerch, Nov. 6, 1844.

ANDREW AND MATILDA (BOWMAN) CORTRIGHT, issue:
Fletcher.
Parmelia.
Dingman.
Christian.
Susanna.
Ashbel Morris.
+Jesse D., b. 1819, m. Mary Cortright, m. 2d, Martha Turner.

ELISHA AND SARAH (KLINETOP) CORTRIGHT, issue:
John, Abram, Christopher, Jacob, Margaret, Lydia, Washington,
Anna, Erastus and Ellen.

JOHN B. AND NANCY (SANTEE) CORTRIGHT, issue:
James.
Abram, b. 1829, m. Lucinda Fortner.
Rachel, b. 1832, m. Tobias L. Gardner.

JOHN B. AND ELIZA (POLLOCK) CORTRIGHT, issue:
Nancy Jane.
Sylvester T., m. Margaret Edwards.

ISAAC AND MARY (POLLOCK) CORTRIGHT, issue:
+Elisha D., b. Jan. 3, 1834, m. Margaret Potter, July 4, 1861.
William P., b. Oct. 21, 1835.
+John W., b. Oct. 13, 1837, m. Mary A. Seitz, Sept. 15, 1861.
+Joseph R., b. Mar. 19, 1841, m. Elizabeth Burkett, Oct. 12, 1870.
Richard P., b. Aug. 31, 1843, m. Annetta Simonson, Nov. 22, 1876.
Thomas C., b. May 6, 1846.

Margaret E., b. May 5, 1849, m. John Moore.
+Nathan A., b. Sept. 27, 1852, m. Caroline Burkett, Dec. 9, 1873.
+Frank S., b. Sept. 29, 1854, m. Harriet Trowbridge.

JOSEPH AND LYDIA (KLINETOP) CORTRIGHT, issue:
Richard.

ELISHA AND MARTHA (COLE) CORTRIGHT, issue:
Elias and Huldah.

NATHAN D. AND MARGARETTA (HARLAN) CORTRIGHT, issue:
+Harlan W., b. 1845, m. Eliza Le Fevre.
+Nathan D., b. 1847, m. Margaret S. Kennedy, 1875.
Gertrude M., b. 1849, m. Simon B. Cunningham.
Samuel M., b. 1852, d. 1896.
+William A., b. 1855, m. Jennie Rawlins, 1883.
Emma L., b. 1857, m. Edwin F. Keene.

ABRAM D. AND ELIZABETH (LERCH) CORTRIGHT, issue:
+Milton L., b. Sept. 14, 1846, m. Mary E. Supplee, Dec. 7, 1871.
Mary, b. Mar. 29, 1848, m. Townsend G. Fulmer, 1879.
Arseneth, b. Aug. 14, 1850, m. Eugene D. Boyer, Feb. 1, 1877.
Clara, b. Sept. 25, 1853, m. Morris K. Schweitzer, Aug. 22, 1882.

JESSE D. AND MARTHA (TURNER) CORTRIGHT, issue:
Miner.
Burton.
Alice.
Elizabeth.
+Bowman, m. Laura Kingsbury.

ELISHA D. AND MARGARET (POTTER) CORTRIGHT, issue:
+Joseph D., b. Nov. 17, 1863, m. Nora Mufley.
+Thomas C., b. Sept. 22, 1869, m. Nellie M. Leavenz.
Samuel, b. Oct. 16, 1871.
Nathan D., b. Sept. 4, 1875.
Isaac, b. May 1, 1878.
John M., b. Sept. 19, 1879.
Sarah H., b. May 3, 1882.

JOHN W. AND MARY A. (SEITZ) CORTRIGHT, issue:
Theresa I., b. June 10, 1862, m. William Lough.
+Isaac H., b. June 5, 1867, m. Ada Flint.
May, b. Mar. 26, 1869, m. W. Q. Edson.
William E., b. Aug. 27, 1872.
Anna V., b. Jan. 4, 1874, m. R. W. Perkins.
Flora G., b. Oct. 7, 1875, m. R. W. Dennis.
Laura.
Wilson G., b. June 29, 1877.

JOSEPH R. AND ELIZABETH (BURKETT) CORTRIGHT, issue:

Mollie J., b. Aug. 6, 1871.
Fannie F., b. Oct. 3, 1873.
Grace K., b. Mar. 7, 1877.

Maud B., b. Aug. 19, 1879.
Josephine B., b. Jan. 27, 1882.
Luther.

NATHAN A. AND CATHARINE (BURKETT) CORTRIGHT, issue:

+J. Wilbur, b. Feb. 28, 1876, m. Mary Smith.

Charles N., b. Jan. 1, 1878.
Shelby M., b. Apr. 5, 1880.
Nellie B., b. Jan. 25, 1883.

Clyde C., b. Feb. 1, 1885.
Cecil J., b. Aug. 27, 1888.

FRANK S. AND HARRIET (TROWBRIDGE) CORTRIGHT, issue:
Harlan and Ethel.

HARLAN W. AND ELIZA (LE FEVRE) CORTRIGHT, issue:

Mabel L., b. Dec. 24, 1876.
William L., b. Dec. 3, 1879.

John H., b. Dec. 24, 1886.
Abbie H., b. Feb. 26, 1889.

NATHAN D. AND MARGARET S. (KENNEDY) CORTRIGHT, issue:

Charles, b. 1878.
Frank, b. 1880.
Henry L., b. 1882.

Edgar, b. 1884.
Donald, b. 1889.
Margaret, b. 1895.

WILLIAM A. AND JENNIE (RAWLINS) CORTRIGHT, issue:

Nannie R., b. May 9, 1885.
Edwin K., b. Jan. 18, 1887.
Nathan D., b. Jan. 1, 1890.

William A., b. Apr. 12, 1893.
James, b. Mar. 11, 1896.
Frances W., b. Oct. 17, 1898.

MILTON L. AND MARY (SUPPLEE) CORTRIGHT, issue:

Grace P., b. Sept. 11, 1872.
Robert M., b. Dec. 29, 1877.

Florence T., b. Dec. 10, 1881.

BOWMAN AND LAURA (KINGSBURY) CORTRIGHT, issue:
Lawrence.

ISAAC H. AND ADA (FLINT) CORTRIGHT, issue:
Emma.

J. WILBUR AND MARY (SMITH) CORTRIGHT, issue:
Vernon S.

JOSEPH D. AND NORA (MUFLEY) CORTRIGHT, issue:
Archie and Carl I.

THOMAS AND NELLIE (LEAVENZ) CORTRIGHT, issue:
Blanche M.

ALLIED FAMILIES

THE KENNEDY, VAN VLIET, SWARTWOUT AND ALLIED FAMILIES.

JOHN KENNEDY, born April 24, 1739, who came from Bangor, County Down, Ireland, prior to 1762, and settled near Kingston, Ulster County, New York, is the first of this family of whom there is knowledge.

He was of the Scotch Presbyterian faith, and lived near the Kennedy family of Cultra, Ireland, and is supposed to be related to it.

Family tradition assures us that John Kennedy, a tailor by trade, was a man of ability, clear headed and kind hearted.

Soon after coming to America, he enlisted April 6, 1762, as a soldier of the New York Provincial troops, under Capt. James Clinton, the muster roll stating his age twenty-three years, born in Ireland, a "taylor" by trade, stature, five feet, six inches.

He also was on the muster roll of troops raised to guard the western frontiers of Ulster and Orange Counties, enlisting Nov. 24, 1763, and on a list of Officers in Florida and Warwick, Orange Co., in Capt. Nathaniel Elmer's Company, and was appointed second Lieut., his name being written John Cannadee.

During the Revolution, he served as a private in the 4th Regiment, Orange County, N. Y., Militia, at that time, a resident there; on Sept. 24, 1781, he enlisted in the Company commanded by Anthony Crotser, and was in actual service on the frontiers of Northampton County, Pa., and also was a soldier of the first class in the 3d Company, 4th Battalion, Northampton County Militia, May 14, 1781, and on Sept. 24, same year, enlisted in Capt. Lerk's Company of Militia, in the service of the frontier under Lieut. Christian Shouse.

He afterward removed to the Wyoming Valley, settling at Plains, where he bought a farm, on which he lived until his death, Aug. 20, 1809.

About 1764, he m. Maria Van Vliet, of Orange County, and had issue:

Catharine, b. July 22, 1766, m. Cornelius Cortright, Oct. 1, 1786.
James, bap. Sept. 29, 1768, m. Sarah Abbott.
John, m. Nancy Armstrong.
Elizabeth, b. Apr. 12, 1773, m. James Stark, Nov. 3, 1791.
Thomas, bap. June 22, 1783, m. Elizabeth Schofield, 1801.

ADRIAEN GERRITSEN VAN VLIET, a farmer, came from Utrecht, in Holland, in the ship "Faith," May 24, 1662, with wife and five children, aged 13, 12, 11, 8 and 7. His wife was Agatha Jans Spruyt, of an old family of Kriekenbeck and Opstal, in the province of Utrecht.

He is first named at Kingston, as a witness June 5, 1663, and took the oath of allegiance in 1669. His name, Van Vliet, means in Dutch, "of the stream, or channel," and written in early church records, Van Vlied. He spent his life in Kingston, after his arrival, having had the following children, all born in Holland:

Machtel, m. Barent Van Borsom, m. 2d, Jan Jacob Stol, in 1684.
Geertje, m. Gysbert Crom, before 1677.
Gerrit, m. Pieternelle Swart, before 1681.
+Jan, m. Judith Hussey, Oct. 4, 1684.
Dirck, m. Anna Andriessen, Apr. 23, 1685.

JAN VAN VLIET was born in the "Stigt van Utrecht," came with his parents in 1662, and lived at Kingston. His wife was the daughter of Frederick and Margaret Hussey, and was bap. at Kingston, Oct. 9, 1667.

Frederick Hussey was an English soldier, one of twenty-five sent by Gov. Nichols to Kingston to protect the settlers there, soon after the Indian massacre in 1663; he was granted land at Kingston in 1668, and at Marbletown in 1669, where he afterward resided. His name was written in the Kingston church records variously as Hussei, Hossey, Horsjes, etc.

Jan and Judith (Hussey) Van Vliet had issue:

Achie, bap. Jan. 31, 1686, m. Joost Hoornbeek, Oct. 28, 1707.
Frederick, m. Mary Biggs, Nov. 22, 1718.
Margrietje, m. Gerrit Konstapel, before 1721.
+Jan, bap. Nov. 16, 1694, m. Jesyntjen Swartwout, Mar. 11, 1725.
Ari, bap. Jan. 31, 1697, m. Lena Roosekrans, before 1734.
Willem, bap. June 4, 1699, m. Sara Van Keuren, Nov. 10, 1726.
Debora, bap. Oct. 12, 1701, m. Petrus Louw, before 1737.
Geertje, bap. Sept. 3, 1704, m. Christoffel Van Bommel, June 21, 1725.
Anna, bap. June 24, 1711, m. Johannes Keter, before 1731.

JAN VAN VLIET, m. at Kingston, Mar. 11, 1725, Jesyntjen Swartwout; he was born in Marbletown, which he left about 1725 with his family, being one of the earliest settlers in the Minisink (Peenpack patent), in Orange County, New York, where he was a farmer, an elder in the Dutch church at Machackemeck (Deerpark), and a prominent and respected man.

After the death of his first wife, he m. 2d, Leya Decker, widow of John Williams, May 19, 1757. By his wife, Jesyntjen Swartwout, issue:

Samuel, bap. May 8, 1726, m. Tjatje Cole, Nov. 26, 1752.
Benjamin, bap. Jan. 28, 1728, m. Johanna Westfal Apr. 16, 1757, m. 2d, Grietje Decker, Jan. 2, 1763.
Elizabeth, bap. about 1730, m. Daniel Gonsales, July 10, 1750.
Daniel, bap. Feb. 4, 1733, m. Sara Cuddeback, Dec. 8, 1752.
Jacobus, bap. Oct. 30, 1739, m. Margaret Palmetier.
+Maria, bap. Apr. 14, 1743, m. John Kennedy, before 1766.
Catharina, bap. Apr. 23, 1747, m. Benjamin Cuddeback, about 1767.
By his second wife, Leya Decker, he had issue:
Jesyntje, bap. Jan. 28, 1759, m. Jacobus Cuddeback, before 1781.

Owing to differences as to Coetus and Conferentie, (i. e. church jurisdiction), Maria was baptized again, June 21, 1747, the same sponsors, Jacob Westbroek and Maria Westbroek, serving, and probably she was named for the latter.

THOMAS SWARTWOUT was a native of Groningen, Holland, where he m. June 3, 1631, Hendrickje Barents, his second wife, with whom he came at an early date, and after several years residenced elsewhere, he finally settled in Albany. His son,

ROELOF SWARTWOUT, was baptized in the Oude-kerk, Amsterdam, Holland, June 1, 1634, came to New Amsterdam in 1655, and settled at Ft. Orange. He returned to Holland in 1660, and returning, brought with him an appointment from the Directors of the Dutch West India Company, dated April 15, 1660, as Schout (sheriff or magistrate) at Wiltwyck, (Kingston), and on the establishment of the Court there, he was appointed the first Schout, May 23, 1661, by Gov. Stuyvesant, with authority to act as Judge and decide cases, where for several years he acted as such, and later, was appointed Justice and collector of the Grand Excise, and died May, 1715.

He married at Ft. Orange, (Albany) Aug. 13, 1657, Eva Alberts, Bratt (Bradt) widow of Anthony de Hooges, and had issue:

Hendrickje, b. about 1658, m. Huibert Lambertsen Brink, Mar. 18, 1679.
Thomas, b. about 1660, m. Lysbet Gardenier, about 1682.
Antoni, bap. May 11, 1664, m. Jannetje Jacobus, Apr. 30, 1693.
Cornelia, bap. Mar. 13, 1667, m. Hendrick Claes Schoonmaker, before 1689.
Rachel, bap. Apr. 10, 1669, m. Jacob Kip, before 1695.
Eva, m. Jacob Dingemans, Oct. 9, 1698.
Bernardus, bap. Apr. 26, 1673, m. Rachel Schepmoes, May 19, 1700.

In his will dated March 30, 1714, he gives Thomas twenty-five pounds, his right as being his first born son, his children Hendrickje, Rachel, and Eva each sixty-five pounds, the same to the children of Anthony and Cornelia, deceased, and his entire estate in Ulster County to his sons, Thomas and Bernardus, upon certain conditions.

THOMAS SWARTWOUT, of Kingston, was probably born there about 1660, and being the eldest son, named after his paternal grandfather.

On Oct. 14, 1697, a patent for about 1200 acres of land, located at Peenpack, Orange County, New York, in the Minisink, was granted to him, his brothers, Antoni and Bernardus, Jan Tysen, Peter Guimar, David Jamison and Jacob Cobebec, but he does not appear to have ever settled there.

He m. Lysbet Gardenier about 1682, and had issue:

Jacobus, bap. Apr. 17, 1692, m. Gieletjen Nieukerk, Oct. 5, 1714.
Eva, bap. Nov. 16, 1694, m. Frederick Schoonmaker, Feb. 6, 1717.
Rudolphus, bap. Mar. 28, 1697, m. Sarah ——.
Jesyntjen bap. Aug. 13, 1699, m. Jan Van Vliet, Mar. 11, 1725.
Samuel, bap. Jan. 22, 1702, m. Elizabeth Guimar.
Also Roelof, Josyna and Roulof, who died young.

ALBERT ANDRIES BRATT, "Noorman," and wife, Annetje Barents Van Rotmers, were from Frederickstad, Norway, who sailed from Amsterdam, Holland, Sept. 25, 1636, in the "Arms of Rensselaerswyck," being a young couple, as it appears from Killian Van Rensselaer's journal of his administration as patroon.

Their ship spent about a week at Ilfracombe, England, on the Bristol Channel, arrived at New York in March, and finally at Albany (Beverswyck) on April 7th, 1637.

He died June 7th, 1686, and the chronicler (Swartwout) who recorded his death, took pains to state he was "one of the earliest dwellers in the Colony of Rensselaerswyck."

His wife, Annetje Barents Van Rotmers, died in 1662, and on July 10th, 1663, her children gave Storm, Albertsen, her eldest son, power of attorney to collect property inherited from Pieter Jacobson Van Rynsburgh, husband of their maternal grandmother, Geesje Barents, who came as early as 1642.

Albert Andries and Annetje Barents (Van Rotmers) Bratt had several children, among whom, Eva Alberts Bratt, who m. 1st Anthony de Hooges, and m. 2d, Roelof Swartwout, Aug. 13, 1657.

JACOB JANSEN GARDENIER (ALIAS FLODDER), a carpenter, and wife Josyna, (her name unrecovered) were in Beverswyck as early as 1638.

In 1656 he owned the north side of Wall Street, from William to Pearl Street, which he divided and sold. He early bought land in Kinderhook, together with the Goyer's Kill opposite Apje's Island, or Shotack.

Josyna died in Feb., 1669, and he m. 2d, Barentje Stratsman, having had several children by his first wife, among whom, Lysbet, who m. Thomas Swartwout, about 1682.

THE BAILEY, GORE, PARK AND ALLIED FAMILIES.

JOHN BAILEY, who m. Lydia, daughter of Thomas Smith, of Haddam, Conn., was a viewer of chimneys and ladders at Hartford, Conn., in 1648, constable in March, 1656, and made freeman in May, 1657.

He removed to Haddam about 1662, as one of the 28 original purchasers. His will was dated June 17, 1696, and the inventory taken Aug. 29, 1697, amounted to 186 pounds, 10 shillings, 6 pence. He lived at Higganum, in the northern part of Haddam. His son,

JOHN BAILEY, of Haddam, m. Elizabeth Bate, daughter of John and Elizabeth (Beckwith) Bate, and died Jan. 15, 1718. His son,

JOHN BAILEY, of Haddam, born Oct. 1688, m. Esther ——, Jan. 14, 1711, leaving a son,

JEREMIAH BAILEY, born Aug. 14, 1718, m. ——, who had a son,

JEREMIAH BAILEY, born about 1740, at Preston, Conn., married in 1763, Hannah Parks, a school teacher, the parents of

BENJAMIN BAILEY, born Nov. 7, 1768, at Norwich, Conn., m. Lydia, daughter of Lieut. Daniel and Mary (Parks) Gore, Nov. 27, 1794; he made a study of music, and was engaged in teaching same for some time.

He removed to the Wyoming Valley, buying land at Plains Township, where he engaged in farming, also operating a tannery, and raised a large family of children. His name appears on the muster roll of Westmoreland Militia, belonging to the 24th Regiment, having served two months and five days prior to Oct. 1st, 1778, from June 28th 1778. He died at Abington, Luzerne County, Pa., May 2, 1858, leaving issue:

Sidney, b. Nov. 22, 1795, m. Laura Shaw.
Benjamin F., b. Oct. 14, 1797, m. Catharine Stark, May 20, 1821.
Benajah P., b. Nov. 26, 1799, m. Parma Parsons, Jan. 4, 1821, m. 2d, Martha Pierce.
Caroline, b. Feb. 10, 1802, m. Jeremiah Smith, May 18, 1819.

Hannah, b. Oct. 8, 1803, m. Samuel Wilcox.
Harriet, b. Dec. 2, 1805, m. Cornelius L. Courtright, July 10, 1827.
Avery W., b. July 7, 1808, m. Lydia Atwood.
Milton, b. Feb. 13, 1812, m. Loduskia Lane, m. 2d, Fanny Andrus.
Daniel G., b. Apr. 22, 1815, m. Maria Stott.

John Gore, the pioneer ancestor of the family, and first of the name to emigrate to New England, came from Waltham Abbey, Sussex, England, where he was born, and died in Roxbury, Mass., June 2, 1657.

He came to Roxbury, with his wife Rhoda, on April 18, 1637, and was one of the few men designated as "mister." He is mentioned in a list of land owners of the year 1643, as owning 143 acres. When he landed at Boston and passed on Boston Neck to Roxbury, "Mrs. Gore was carried by two men, as the ground was wet and swampy. Arriving at Roxbury, the men stopped with their fair burden on a small hill, when Mrs. Gore, who was much fatigued, exclaimed, this is Paradise, and thereafter, the spot was named Paradise Hill."

John Gore was a member of the Ancient and Honorable Artillery Company, 1638, clerk of the Company, 1655, and for many years served as town clerk, the records of Roxbury, now in the city hall, Boston, being in his handwriting, and in that of his son, who succeeded him.

In the church, "Mr. Gore's pew was located by the pulpit stairs;" his homestead was situated on the west side of Tremont Street, just beyond the Providence railroad crossing, extending to Parker's Street, and the old house was torn down in 1876.

Upon his death, his estate inventoried 812 pounds; by his wife Rhoda, he had eleven children, among them,

Samuel, born 1652, a carpenter by trade, who served as selectman for several years, and died July 4, 1692. He m. Aug. 28, 1672, Elizabeth, daughter of John and Margaret (Bowen) Weld, son of Capt. Joseph Weld, of Roxbury.

He was Lieutenant in the Military Company of Roxbury in 1689, which took part in the revolution that overthrew the government of Sir Edmund Andros; was one of the original twelve proprietors of the Mashamoquet Purchase, afterward Pomfret, Windham County, Conn., granted them in October, 1687. He had several children, among them,

Samuel Gore, born in Roxbury, Oct. 20, 1681. He m. Hannah, a daughter of Moses and Hannah (Chandler) Draper, and granddaughter of James and Miriam (Stansfield) Draper, also of John and Elizabeth (Douglas) Chandler, in 1703, and died May 27, 1756, his wife, July 11, 1741.

Early in the 18th century, subsequently to 1704, with his family, he removed from Roxbury to Norwich, Conn., where he continued to reside until his death. In May, 1721, he was commissioned Captain of the 5th Company, Connecticut Militia, located in Norwich.

Capt. Samuel and Hannah (Draper) Gore had nine children, the sixth,

OBADIAH GORE, born at Norwich, July 26, 1714, learned the trade of a blacksmith, and settled in his native town. He m. Hannah, daughter of Thomas and Hannah (Witter) Park, Nov. 4, 1742, who was second in descent from Thomas and Mary (Allyn) Park, and Josiah and Sarah (Crandall) Witter; third from Thomas and Dorothy (Thompson) Park, Robert Allyn, William Witter, and Rev. John and Hannah Crandall; fourth from John Thompson, and Robert Park.

In May, 1761, Obadiah Gore was commissioned Ensign of the 8th Company, of the 3d Regiment, Connecticut Militia; May 1762, promoted Lieutenant of the same Company, and in May, 1766, was commissioned Captain of the same.

He and his father early became members of the Susquehannah Company and as owners of one share each, their names appear as grantees in the Indian deed of July 11, 1754.

He was a member of the Committee of Settlers at Wyoming in June, 1770, so about this time he first came to the Wyoming Valley, as his name frequently appears, and it is evident that up to the time of his death, he was active and prominent in Wyoming affairs.

In May, 1777, and again in May, 1778, he was commissioned by Gov. Jonathan Trumbull, one of the Justices of the Peace for the County of Westmoreland, for the year ensuing.

He resided in Kingston, and in the tax lists for 1776, he was rated at 68 pounds, 18 shillings, for that district. When the battle of Wyoming was fought, Capt. Gore was one of the small company of old men who remained in Forty Fort for its defense, and five of his sons, and two sons-in-law marched out with the patriots to meet the invading British and Indians, and of these seven, five fell on the field of battle.

He died of small pox, Jan. 10, 1779, and his wife died at Sheshequin, Pa., Aug. 14, 1804, in her 84th year. Their issue:

Obadiah, b. Apr. 7, 1744, m. Mar. 22, 1764, Anna Avery. He was a
    very prominent man, serving as Judge, Lieut. in the Revolution,
    a member of the Legislature, etc.; d. Mar. 22, 1821.
Daniel, b. Mar. 13, 1746, mentioned hereafter.

Silas, b. Dec. 23, 1747, killed by Indians, July 3, 1778; m. Kessiah
Yarrington, 1770.

Asa, b. Feb. 28, 1750, killed in battle of Wyoming, July 3, 1778; m.
Elizabeth Avery, 1777.

Hannah, b. May 28, 1752; m. Timothy Pierce, 1772, who was killed
in the battle, and m. 2d, Thomas Duane.

Lucy, b. May 26, 1754, d. Sept. 30, 1820; m. John Murphy, killed in
the battle, July 3, 1778.

Sarah, b. Nov. 23, 1756; d. May 1841; m. Lieut. Lawrence Myers,
Jan. 2, 1782; m. 2d, Benjamin Bidlack, Apr. 15, 1811.

George, b. Sept. 1, 1759, killed in battle of Wyoming, July 3, 1778.

Samuel, b. May 24, 1761, d. May 2, 1834; m. Sarah Brokaw, 1785.

John, b. Feb. 25, 1764, d. Aug. 4, 1837; m. Elizabeth Ross, 1793.

DANIEL GORE, second son of Capt. Obadiah and Hannah (Park)
Gore, was born at Norwich, Conn., Mar. 13, 1746, and died at Plains,
Luzerne County, Pa., Sept. 3, 1809.

He married Mary, daughter of Adam and Lydia (Tracy) Park, born
Aug. 2, 1737, the date of his marriage not being recorded.

In his 17th year (1763), he came to Wyoming with the original settlers, and returning to Norwich, learned the trade of a blacksmith, and
came again to Wyoming in the spring of 1769.

He assisted in the erection of Fort Durkee, and was one of its in-
mates when, in Nov., 1769, it was surrendered to the Pennamites, and
the Yankees were required to depart from the Valley.

He returned to Wyoming in 1770, and at the original allotment of
lands in the town-plot of Wilkes-Barre, drew lot number 20.

When, in January, 1771, Fort Durkee was captured a second time by
the Pennamites, Daniel Gore was one of the Yankees who were taken
prisoners, and sent to Philadelphia, where they were confined for several
months. Returning to his home in Connecticut, June, 1771, he immediately marched for Wyoming with his brothers, Obadiah, Silas, and Asa, in
the Company of Yankees commanded by Capt. Butler, to besiege the
Pennamites.

When in 1772, the final distribution of lands in Wilkes-Barre was
made, he drew, among other lots, Meadow lot No. 38, and subsequently
acquired the adjoining lot, No. 37. These lots contained about sixty-six
acres, and lay along the Susquehanna River, on Jacobs Plains, in what
is now Plains Township, nearly opposite the site of Forty Fort.

Here, subsequently, he established his home and lived—except when
driven away by the Pennamites and Indians—until his death.

Miner (in his *History of Wyoming*) has recorded the following concerning the part he took in the battle of Wyoming: "Lieut. Daniel Gore

was near the right wing, and stood a few rods below Wintermoot's Fort, close to the old road that led up through the valley. Stepping into the road, a ball struck him in the arm, and tearing it from his shirt, he applied a hasty bandage. Just at that moment Capt. (Robert) Durkee stepped into the road at the same place. 'Look out,' cried Lieut. Gore.

At that instant a bullet struck Capt. Durkee in the thigh. When retreat became inevitable, Lieut. Gore endeavored to assist Capt. Durkee from the field, but found it impossible, and Capt. Durkee said, 'Save yourself, Mr. Gore—my fate is sealed.' Lieut. Gore then escaped down the road and leaping a fence about a mile below, lay under a bunch of bushes, and after dark, found his way to the Fort." Escaping from the Valley with other fugitives, he returned to Wilkes-Barre, in August, 1778, and taking command of a small remnant of the Militia company, formed a part of the force at Wyoming, under the command of Col. Zebulon Butler.

He had been commissioned by Governor Trumbull, October, 1775, Lieutenant of the 6th Company, 24th Regiment, Connecticut Militia, which took part in the battle of Wyoming. He continued in the Military service at Wilkes-Barre as Lieutenant until the Sullivan expedition set out for New York, when he accompanied it, returning home with it in October, 1779.

In November, 1787, he was elected Captain of the Upper Wilkes-Barre Company, in the Battalion of Luzerne County Militia, commanded by Lieut. Col. Matthias Hollenback.

He died at his home at Plains, Sept. 3, 1809, and his wife died Apr. 11, 1806; their remains lie in the little graveyard near Port Bowkley, now surrounded by culm piles.

Daniel Gore and his brother, Obadiah, who were blacksmiths, were the first to use Anthracite coal, then called black rock, which they did in their forges when they came to Wyoming in 1769, finding by experiment that when ignited, and fanned by an air blast, it gave greater satisfaction than heating iron by the use of wood, formerly the custom.

To Judge Jesse Fell, however, must be given the credit for first using coal as a fuel for heating in grates, as he and his nephew, Edward Fell, made an open grate, and set it in the fire place of his home, Feb. 11, 1808. He invited several of the neighbors to witness the test, but only two came, for fear of being hoaxed.

He made this entry on the flyleaf of his "Treatise on Masonry," Feb. 11, of Masonry, 5808; Made the "Experment" of burning the common coal of this valley in a grate, in a common fire-place in my house, and find it will answer the purpose of fuel, making a cleaner and better fire at less expense, than burning wood in the common way.

Lieut. Daniel and Mary (Park) Gore had issue:

Lydia, b. May 7, 1768, m. Benjamin Bailey, Nov. 27, 1794.
Theresa, b. Feb. 11, 1771, d. May 5, 1854, m. 1st, Aaron Clark, m. 2d, Samuel Carey.
Rachel, b. Mar. 23, 1773, m. Henry Cortright, about 1798.
Polly, m. Silas Smith.
Daniel, b. Jan. 29, 1777, d. Dec. 22, 1839, m. Clarinda Capron, Dec. 28, 1800.
George, b. 1781, d. May, 1856, m. Mary Larned, m. 2d, Susanna Carey.

ROBERT PARK (OR PARKE), born in Preston, England, 1580, a man of means, sailed with his family from Cowes, Isle of Wight, on the ship "Arabella," and landed in Boston, Mar. 29, 1630. He was of Cambridge, 1635, Wethersfield, 1635 to 1649, and Deputy to the General Court, 1641 to 1642; removed to New London, Conn., in 1649 where he lived six years, his barn being the first place of worship there. He finally settled at Mystic, in Stonington, and was selectman in 1658; he served in the early Colonial wars, and m. 1st, in England, Martha Chaplin, and 2d, May 30, 1644, Mrs. Alice Thompson, widow of John Thompson. His will was dated May 14, 1660, and he died Feb. 4, 1664, leaving children by his first wife, William, Thomas and Samuel.

THOMAS PARK, born Preston, Lancashire, England, came in 1630, was of Wethersfield in 1639, where he married Dorothy, dau. of John and Alice Thompson. About 1650, he removed to New London, becoming Deacon in the church, and in 1681, collector of taxes. In 1698, with his sons Robert and John, and nine others, he organized the First Church of Preston, Conn., becoming the first deacon. He came to Preston about 1680, served in the Colonial wars, and died July 30, 1709, aged ninety years, having had:

Martha Park, b. Oct. 27, 1646, d. Feb. 14, 1717, m. Isaac Wheeler, 1667.
Thomas Park, b. Apr. 18, 1648, m. Mary, dau. of Robert Allyn, Jan. 4, 1671; received from the town a considerable grant of land, and had:
Samuel Park, b. Nov. 26, 1673, m. Abigail, dau. of —— Avers, May 8, 1709.
Thomas Park, b. Jan. 20, 1676, m. Hannah, dau. of Josiah and Sarah (Crandall) Witter, and granddaughter of William Witter and John Crandall, the latter a follower of Roger

Williams, ordered to leave the colony by the Puritans, and one of the founders of Warwick, R. I.

Samuel and Abigail (Ayers) Park had a son,

Adam Park, b. July 31, 1714, m. May 18, 1832, Lydia, dau. of Christopher Tracy, who m. Lydia Parish in 1705; granddau. of Johnathan and Mary (Griswold) Tracy and John and Mary (Wattell) Parish; 3d in descent from Lieut. Thomas Tracy, Lieut. Francis Griswold, John Wattell; 4th from Edward Griswold.

Thomas and Hannah (Witter) Park had issue:

Benajah Park, b. July 8, 1718, m. May 20, 1741, Lydia Parish, b. Sept. 16, 1719, the dau. of William and Jerusha (Smith) Parish; granddau. of John and Mary (Wattell) Parish, and 3d from John Wattell.

Hannah Park, (sister of Benajah) b. June 22, 1721, m. Capt. Obadiah Gore, Nov. 4, 1742.

Adam and Lydia (Tracy) Park had a daughter:

Mary Park, b. Aug. 20, 1737, d. Apr. 11, 1806, m. Lieut. Daniel Gore.

Benajah and Lydia (Parish) Park had a daughter:

Hannah Park, b. Feb. 14, 1743, m. about 1763, Jeremiah Bailey.

THE ABBOTT, SEARLE, FULLER, MOULTON AND ALLIED FAMILIES.

There were several families by the name of Abbott who came to New England at a very early day, all supposed to be more or less distantly related, but the connection has never been proven. The compiler of the Abbott family of Andover, says, "my opinion, but I have no authority for it, is that the early Abbotts of Andover and other places were all descended from Sir Thomas Abbott, of Easington, England, who flourished early in the sixteenth century." He also says:

"GEORGE ABBOTT, the venerable ancestor of a numerous progeny, was born in England, 1615, who emigrated from Yorkshire in 1637, coming over in the same ship with his future wife, and lived several years at Roxbury. In 1643 he went to Andover, Mass., there becoming one of the first settlers and original proprietors, his house being a garrison to protect the settlers from attacks by the Indians, used as such during his life, and for many years after his death, Dec. 24, 1681, O. S., aged 66 years. He married Hannah, dau. of William and Annis Chandler, Dec. 12, 1646, and with Christian submission, they endured their trials, dangers, and privations, of which they had a large share; they were industrious, economical, sober, pious and respected, Puritans in faith, and brought up a family of thirteen children well, trained them in the way they should go, from which they did not depart." He made his will Dec. 12, 1681, proved Mar. 28, 1682, in which he pays a fine tribute to his wife, who after his death, m. Rev. Francis Dane, minister at Andover, whom she survived, and died June 11, 1711.

WILLIAM ABBOTT, born Nov. 18, 1657, was a weaver by trade, who spent his entire life at Andover, where he m. June 19, 1682, Elizabeth, dau. of Nathaniel and Ann (Douglas) Geary (or Geere), and granddau. of Denis Geary and William and Ann (Mattle) Douglas.

He died Oct. 21, 1713, his wife Nov. 26, 1712, both being also Puritans in faith and Christian conduct, leaving twelve children, of whom;

PHILIP ABBOTT, born at Andover, Apr. 3, 1699, a farmer, removed to Hampton, Conn., about 1722, later settling at Windham, where he married Abigail Bickford, Oct. 20, 1723, and where his children were born. He was chosen deacon of the second church in Windham, Apr. 25, 1739. He died April 17, 1749, his estate being partially settled in the probate court, Oct. 8, 1749. They had issue:

John, b. July 12, 1724, d. July 18, 1740.
Abiel, b. Mar. 3, 1726, m. Abigail Fenton.
Stephen, b. Apr. 21, 1728, m. Freelove Burgess.
Hannah, b. Mar. 16, 1730, m. Samuel Utley, 1748.
Mary, b. July 6, 1732, m. Capt. Stephen Fuller, Oct. 17, 1751.
Joseph, b. Feb. 14, 1735, m. Elizabeth Stedman, and 2d, Olive Pearce.
John, 2d, b. Sept. 27, 1741, m. Alice Fuller, sister of Stephen, who m. after the death of her husband, Stephen Gardner, of Plains, Pa.

JOHN ABBOTT, born Sept. 27, 1741, at Hampton, Windham County, Conn., married at Hampton, (parish of Canada), Nov. 4, 1762, Alice Fuller, a daughter of Stephen Fuller, Sen., and coming to the Wyoming Valley early in March, 1772, he soon afterward executed a "settlers" bond. Having been admitted a proprietor in Wilkes-Barre, he participated in the distribution of lots, April, 1772, being allotted lot No. 35 in the town plot, lot No. 48 in the first division, lot No. 10 in the third division and lot No. 2 in the fourth division. He first lived in the Fort or blockhouse at Wilkes-Barre until 1774, when, having erected a house on one of his lots in what is now Plains Township, opposite Forty-Fort, he removed there. With his brother-in-law, Capt. Stephen Fuller, he erected the first dwelling in Wilkes-Barre, on the south-west corner of Main and Northampton Streets, which then, in 1772, was a "sterile plain covered with pitch pine and scrub oak." He took part in the battle of Wyoming, July 3, 1778, as a private in the 6th, or upper Wilkes-Barre Company, of the

24th Regiment, Connecticut Militia, commanded by Capt. Resin Geer; escaping from the field of battle in the general rout, he waded through the shallow water of the Susquehanna, to Monoconock Island; crossing the Island, being unable to swim, he was aided over the deep channel of the river by his neighbor and fellow soldier, George Cooper, also fleeing from the scene of carnage and desolation. He took his family down the river to Sunbury, and leaving them there, joined the detachment of Militia under the command of Lieut. Col. Zebulon Butler, on August 4th, 1778.

Stone says (*History of Wyoming*) that "Mr. Abbott found his house and barn had been burnt, his cattle slaughtered, or driven away, and his fields ravaged, the gleanings only remaining. These he attempted to gather (about the middle of August) and while in the field with Isaac Williams, a youth of eighteen, they were shot by a party of Indians, who stole upon them unawares, scalped and left dead upon the spot."

His widow, with nine small children, being now entirely destitute, was compelled to seek her way to Hampton, Connecticut, a distance of more than three hundred miles—on foot, penniless, heart broken, and dependent on charity for subsistence. The journey was safely made, and with her family, she remained for several years, until the troubles in Wyoming were over, and her sons grown up, when she returned to the Valley, successfully reclaimed the estate of her husband, upon which she settled."

On Sept. 20, 1782, her brother, Capt. Stephen Fuller, was appointed administrator of the estate of John Abbott, deceased.

Alice Fuller, born Feb. 20, 1741, wife of John Abbott, was a daughter of Stephen and Hannah (Moulton) Fuller; 2d in descent from Thomas and Martha (Durgy) Fuller, and Robert and Hannah (Grove) Moulton; 3d, from Lieut. Thomas and Elizabeth (Tidd) Fuller, William and Martha (Cross) Durgy, Robert and Mary (Cook) Moulton, Nicholas and Hannah (Sallows) Grove; 4th, from John Tidd (or Tead), Robert and Anne (Jordan) Cross, Robert and Abigail (Goode) Moulton, Henry and Judith (Birdsall) Cook, Robert and Freeborn (Wolfe) Sallows; 5th, from Stephen Jordan, Robert Moulton, Micha Sallows, and Peter Wolfe. John and Alice (Fuller) Abbott had issue:

Alice, b. Apr. 17, 1764, m. Amos Utley.
Charles, b. June 3, 1769, m. Urania Manville.
Stephen, b. Apr. 19, 1771; m. Abigail Searle, July 14, 1799.
Abigail, no record.
Reuben, no record.
Lydia, b. June 18, 1775; d. June 13, 1862, m. Artemas Swetland.
Celinda, d. Apr. 16, 1807; m. Reuben Taylor, June 27, 1790.

Mary, b. Oct. 14, 1776; m. John Cortright, Dec. 10, 1800.
Hannah, b. Oct. 14, 1776.
Sarah, b. Feb. 28, 1778, m. James Kennedy.

CHARLES ABBOTT and his wife, Urania Manville, sold the property inherited from the estate of his father, and removed to Sunbury, Ohio, where he died Sept. 1, 1853, and his wife, Dec. 21, 1848, aged 73 years, and 8 months, both buried in Sunbury, Ohio. They had issue:

Charles, d. Dec. 8, 1845, aged 42 years, unm.
Caroline.
Lyman, d. 1870; m. Millie Nicewarner, and lived near Sunbury, Ohio.
Urania, m. George Still, and moved west.
Eliza, m. William Stanton, of Marshalltown, Iowa.

STEPHEN AND ABIGAIL (SEARLE) ABBOTT, see following record:

ARTEMAS AND LYDIA (ABBOTT) SWETLAND, issue:

Augustus, b. Oct. 9, 1797, m. Hannah E. Rich, June 28, 1826, and had:
Delia M., b. Dec. 18, 1832; m. Alfred Barnes, Nov. 22, 1854.
Sarah W., b. May 10, 1834; m. Edward Bliss, Nov. 21, 1856.
Franklin, b. Aug. 4, 1839; m. Matilda Woodruff, Aug. 24, 1867.
Giles T., b. Aug. 19, 1799, m. Sarah Lewis, in 1822, and had:
Byram L., b. Sept. 4, 1824; m. Rachel Swetland.
Joseph C., b. June 5, 1828; m. Martha Gordon, m. 2d, Mary Stauble.
Emily, b. Oct. 6, 1830; m. J. C. Helt, July 3, 1848.
Warren, b. Apr. 24, 1838; m. Margaret Thomas, Feb. 1, 1857.
William L., b.——; m. Cornelia Hults.
Fuller M., b. Sept. 9, 1801, m. Elizabeth Russell, Mar. 8, 1832, and had:
Oliver H. P., b. Apr. 28, 1833.
Livonia C., b. July 4, 1836; m. A. J. Westbrook, Nov. 24, 1859.
Lanora E., b. Feb. 13, 1846; m. William C. Emery.
Seth, b. Mar. 14, 1807, m. Phoebe Lyon, Jan. 16, 1833, and had:
Lydia Ann, b. Dec. 29, 1833; m. William Roberts, May 3, 1851.
Mary L., b. June 25, 1837; m. Dennis Parsons.
Marilla, b. Sept. 14, 1810; m. William Shur, Dec. 6, 1832, and had:
Artemas, m. Hannah I. Wetherbee.
Columbus, m. Constance Welch.

JOHN AND MARY (ABBOTT) CORTRIGHT, see John Cortright, No. 8 for her descendants.

REUBEN AND CELINDA (ABBOTT) TAYLOR, issue:

John Abbott, m. (?), and had:
Stephen, b. 1812, who had: Leonora, b. 1837, and Angelina, b. 1844.

HOME OF STEPHEN ABBOTT, PLAINS, LUZERNE COUNTY, PA.

Truman, b. 1814, who had: Gertrude and Martha.
Silas, b. 1818, who had: Reuben, John and Theodore.
Cynthia, b. 1820, who m. Gilbert Berry and had: Susan, Celin_da, Charlotte and Rosella.
John M., b. 1823.
Celinda, b. 1825.
Charles, b. 1827.
Henry, b. 1830.
Draper, b. 1832.
Helen, b. 1833.
Benira, b. 1838.

Henry, m. (?), and had: Erastus, b. 1820: Polly, b. 1823; Reuben, b. 1825, and Cornelius, b. 1826.

JAMES AND SARAH (ABBOTT) KENNEDY, issue:

Catherine, b. 1804, m. Lucius Utley, and had: James, Jared, Catharine, Eliza Ann, Hester, Lydia, Charles, John and Mary.
Lyman, b. 1806, m. Mercy Swingle, and had: Mary, James, Abigail, John, Thomas, Jannette and Robert.
John A., b. 1808, m. 1838, Elizabeth Campbell, and had: Louisa, Amos and Annette.

STEPHEN ABBOTT, b. at Hampton, Windham County, Conn., April 19, 1771; m. Abigail Searle, July 14, 1799, d. at Plains, Pa., July 22, 1853, was one of the nine children with whom his widowed mother made her way back to Connecticut after the tragic death of the father at the hands of the savages on his farm at Plains, in August, 1778.

The family remained there until 1798, when Stephen Abbott, accompanied by his cousin, Philip Abbott, their families and several others, returned to his father's home at Plains, where he resided until his death. On Oct. 20, 1801, he and his brother Charles purchased the estate of their father from their mother, Alice Fuller Gardner, and their sisters, Celinda Taylor, Lydia Swetland and Sarah Kennedy.

Here he successfully engaged in farming, and later in life, in selling coal from his property, which provided amply for all his needs.

His wife died June 2, 1842, after which he married Sarah, the daughter of Col. Nathan Dennison, and widow of Thomas Ferrier.

Abigail Searle, born June 25, 1779, wife of Stephen Abbott, was the daughter of William and Philene (Frink) Searle, and granddaughter of Constant Searle, who was killed in the battle of Wyoming, his wife being Hannah Miner, and of Andrew and Abigail (Billings) Frink; 3d in descent from Nathaniel and Elizabeth (Kinnecutt) Searle, Simeon and Hannah (Wheeler) Miner, Samuel and Margaret (Wheeler) Frink, and Increase and Hannah (Hewitt) Billings; 4th from Nathaniel and Sarah

(Rogers) Searle, John and Elizabeth (Luther) Kinnecutt, Ephraim and Mary (Stevens) Miner, William and Hannah (Gallup) Wheeler, Samuel and Hannah (Miner) Frink, Isaac and Mary (Shepard) Wheeler, Ebenezer and Anna (Comstock) Billings, and Benjamin and Marie (Fanning) Hewitt; 5th from Robert and Deborah Searle, John and Elizabeth (Pabodie) Rogers, Roger and Joanna (Shepardson) Kinnecutt, Hezekiah and Sarah (Butterworth) Luther, Lieut. Ephraim and Hannah (Avery) Miner, Richard and Mary (Lincoln) Stevens, Isaac and Martha (Park) Wheeler, Benadam and Esther (Prentice) Gallup, John and Grace (Stevens) Frink, Rev. Jeremiah and Mary (Wainwright) Shepard, William Billings, Daniel and Paltiah (Elderkin) Comstock, Thomas and Hannah (Palmer) Hewitt, and Edmund and Ellen Fanning; 6th from John and Ann (Churchman) Rogers, William and Elizabeth (Alden) Pabodie, Daniel and Joanna Shepardson, John Luther, Thomas and Grace (Palmer) Miner, James and Joanna (Greenslade) Avery, Nicholas Stevens, Thomas Lincoln, "the miller," Thomas and Mary Wheeler, Thomas and Dorothy (Thompson) Park, Capt. John and Hannah (Lake) Gallup, John and Esther Prentice, John and Mary Frink, Rev. Thomas and Margaret (Borodale) Shepard, Francis and Phillipa Wainwright, William Billings, William and Elizabeth Comstock, John Elderkin, Walter and Rebecca (Short) Palmer; 7th from Thomas Rogers, of the "Mayflower," Hugh Churchman, John and Priscilla (Mullins) Alden, of the "Mayflower," Walter Palmer, Christopher Avery, Robert Park, John and Alice Thompson, John and Margaret (Read) Lake, Valentine and Alice Prentice, and Francis Wainwright, Senior; 8th from William Mullins, or properly, Molines, a French Huguenot, who came over with the Pilgrims from England, on the Mayflower.

Many of these ancestors of Abigail Searle were prominent in the early days of New England, taking part in the Colonial wars, in the government in various capacities, and all did their share of the hard task necessary to establish our country as it now is, so today, their descendants are enjoying the fruits of their labors and hardships.

STEPHEN AND ABIGAIL (SEARLE) ABBOTT had issue:
John, b. at Plains, Apr. 8, 1800, m. Hannah Courtright.
William, b. at Plains, June 19, 1802, m. Eleanor Courtright.
Elizabeth, b. at Plains, Oct. 22, 1806, m. Robert Miner.
Stephen Fuller, b. Plains, July 14, 1809, m. Charlotte Miner.

JOHN ABBOTT, born at Plains, Luzerne Co., Pa., April 8, 1800; married there, Mar. 11, 1830, Hannah, daughter of Squire Cornelius and Catharine (Kennedy) Cortright, died at his home at Plains, Nov. 27, 1861.

He remained on the farm which he afterward inherited from his father, until he became of age, when he went to Mauch Chunk, Pa., and entered the employ of the Lehigh Coal and Navigation Company, but in 1829 he returned to his ancestral home, and there remained successfully engaged in farming until his death; he acquired considerable additional land at Plains, and it is recorded of him that he was a good friend and neighbor, a first rate financier, and a most industrious business man, who deserved and had the confidence and esteem of all those who came in contact with him. John and Hannah (Courtright) Abbott had issue:

Lucy Waller, b. Plains, Nov. 25, 1833, d. Dec. 3, 1914.
Robert Miner, b. Plains, June 15, 1836, m. Caroline Courtright.
Catharine Courtright, b. Dec. 16, 1838, d. Apr. 8, 1894.

WILLIAM ABBOTT, born at Plains, June 19, 1802; married Nov. 2, 1824, Eleanor, daughter of Squire Cornelius and Catherine (Kennedy) Cortright, and died Feb. 9, 1870.

He also remained at Plains for several years, being engaged in farming, but later, he sold his farm there, and with his family, removed to a farm near Mt. Vernon, Knox County, Ohio, in 1855, on which he lived and which he successfully operated until his death, leaving issue:

John Sommerfield, b. Plains, June 18, 1825, m. Mary E. Johnson,
    Feb. 15, 1866.
Lucinda, b. Plains, Sept. 22, 1826, m. Lorenzo Adams; m. 2d, David
    Mead.
Stephen, b. Plains, Sept. 25, 1830, d. Jan. 19, 1866, m. Mary Saylor,
    about 1854.
Cornelius Courtright, b. Plains, Jan. 22, 1833, unm.

ELIZABETH ABBOTT, born at Plains, Oct. 22, 1806, died Aug. 18, 1846; married at Plains, July 3, 1826, Robert Miner, who was a highly respected man, and prominent in the early affairs of the Wyoming Valley. Their surviving issue was:

Charles Abbott Miner, b. Aug. 30, 1830, m. Eliza Ross Atherton.

STEPHEN FULLER ABBOTT, b. at Plains, July 14, 1809; married Charlotte Miner, a daughter of Hon. Charles Miner, of Plains, and died Feb. 11, 1856.

He also was a farmer, a well informed man, and one who stood high in the community where he lived. He had issue:

William Penn, b. Plains, Dec. 31, 1838, m. Lizzie Wyatt, m. 2d, Delia
    Archer.
Asher Miner, b. Plains, Aug. 15, 1841, m. Mary E. Cook, Jan. 6,
    1864.
Stephen Howard, b. Plains, Oct. 24, 1844, d. Sept. 12, 1887.

ROBERT MINER ABBOTT, born at Plains, June 15, 1836, married Caroline, daughter of Cornelius and Harriet (Bailey) Courtright, of Newark, Kendall Co., Ill., on Dec. 29, 1864, and died of old age at his home in Davenport, Iowa, April 14th 1922. He spent his boyhood days on the old Abbott farm at Plains, assisted in the necessary work thereon, and attended school in a building not far from his home, and afterward, with his sisters, was a student at the Wyoming Seminary at Kingston, completing his education at Easton, Pa.

After the death of his father in 1861, he assisted in settling the estate, and in May, 1864, bought for his mother, the residence located on Franklin and Jackson Streets, in Wilkes-Barre, their home for many years.

Soon after, he went to Illinois, where he married, but returned to Plains, living there until the spring of 1866, when he again went West, locating permanently at Davenport, Iowa, where he first engaged in the leather business, and later in the grain business, in which he was highly successful. Several young men in Davenport owe their success in life to the assistance he rendered, holding his memory in high esteem.

Robert Miner and Caroline (Courtright) Abbott had issue:

John Howard, b. at Plains, Feb. 26, 1866; m. Mabel G. Hax.

Carrie Helene, b. Davenport, Ia., Nov. 22, 1867; m. Ira R. Tabor.

Robert Bruce, b. Davenport, Ia., Aug. 18, 1873; m. Teckla Engburgh; m. 2d, Cora A. Engburgh.

JOHN SOMMERFIELD ABBOTT, born at Plains, June 16, 1825, married Mary E. Johnson, Feb. 15, 1866, and died Dec. 23, 1903.

He came to Ohio with his parents at an early day, as did his brother Cornelius, where both engaged in farming near Mt. Vernon, having inherited the estate of their father there.

Both the Abbott brothers were men of standing in the community, highly successful in their undertakings, owning fine farms, and respected for their many excellent qualities.

John Sommerfield and Mary E. (Johnson) Abbott had issue:

Lulu Courtright Abbott, b. Dec. 7, 1866; m. Aug. 23, 1902, Burton D. Herron.

CORNELIUS C. ABBOTT, now retired, lives at Mt. Vernon, where he is surrounded by all to make his declining years comfortable.

HON. CHARLES ABBOTT MINER, born Aug. 30, 1830, at Plains, married Eliza Ross Atherton, Jan. 19, 1853, and died July 25, 1903.

He received his education at the old Wilkes-Barre Academy, and at the Academy at West Chester, Pa., and inherited the flouring mill at

STEPHEN ABBOTT
b. 1771, d. 1853

JOHN ABBOTT
b. 1800, d. 1861

ROBERT MINER ABBOTT
b. 1836, d. 1922

JOHN HOWARD ABBOTT
b. 1866 ——

Miner's Mills, formerly the property of his grandfather, Asher Miner, which business, he followed with marked success.

He was identified with many of Wilkes-Barre's industrial, financial and charitable institutions from early manhood; was elected to the Pennsylvania Legislature in 1874, serving until 1881; was a soldier in the Civil War, enlisting in Company K, 13th Regiment, Penn. Volunteers, in which he held the rank of Sergeant, July 26, 1863; he was known throughout the community where his life was spent, as a benevolent, patriotic, public-spirited man, deeply interested in the welfare of his city.

Charles Abbott and Eliza Ross (Atherton) Miner had surviving issue:

Elizabeth, b. Dec. 18, 1853; d. Nov. 22, 1902.
Asher, b. Nov. 14, 1860; m. Nov. 6, 1889, Hettie McNair Lonsdale.
Sidney Roby, b. July 28, 1864; m. June 25, 1909, Lydia Atherton Stites.
Dr. Charles Howard, b. July 5, 1868; m. June 1, 1904, Grace Lea Shoemaker.

REV. WILLIAM PENN ABBOTT, D. D., born Dec. 31, 1838, married Lizzie Wyatt, Jan. 3, 1860, and after her death, married 2d, Delia Archer, of New York, and died Dec. 22, 1878. He spent his early manhood on the farm at Plains, and becoming interested in religion, entered the ministry of the Methodist Church, where he preached locally with great success. He was also called to other places, where his eloquence bore fruit, and becoming well known for his ability, he went to New York, as Pastor of one of the large churches, where he was greatly esteemed, and his early death regretted by all who knew him.

ASHER MINER ABBOTT, born at Plains, Aug. 15, 1841, married Mary E. Cook, Jan. 6, 1864, and died Mar. 16, 1920, at Minneapolis, Minn.

His education was obtained in the public schools of his home town, and at the West Chester Academy, where it was completed.

When twenty years of age, he enlisted in the Civil War, serving for nearly two years, when he was discharged owing to being injured.

He came to Newark, Ills., about 1864, and to Sandwich, Ills., in 1882, being engaged in business, and retiring in 1896; he was active in church affairs, first becoming a member of the Methodist denomination, and afterward affiliating with the Congregationalists.

He was interested in all that was for the good of the community, lived a life that was above reproach, and was esteemed by all who knew him for his many excellent qualities. He left issue:

Emma Grace, b. Nov. 1, 1864; m. Nov. 21, 1895, Justin Latham.

Elizabeth, b. Apr. 27, 1870; m. June 27, 1894, Dr. Frank E. David.
Sarah, b. Apr. 29, 1873; m. July 25, 1900, Dr. S. Marx White.

JOHN HOWARD ABBOTT, born at Plains, Feb. 26, 1866; married Mabel
G. Hax, June 2, 1913; attended the public schools at Davenport, Iowa,
after which he went to Minneapolis, Minn., engaging in the grain business, removed to Kansas City, Mo., where he became interested in con
struction work in which he is now engaged.

CARRIE HELENE ABBOTT, born at Davenport, Iowa, Nov. 22, 1867;
attended the public schools there, completing her education at St. Cather
ine's, a seminary conducted by the Episcopalian Church. She married
Ira R. Tabor, Nov. 22, 1910, who is an attorney in Davenport, and an
officer in the Episcopal Church, of which both are members.

ROBERT BRUCE ABBOTT, born at Davenport, Aug. 18, 1873; married
Teckla Engburgh, Dec. 29, 1914, and after her death; married 2d, Cora A.
Engburgh, June 21, 1919. He attended the public schools of Davenport,
after which he went to St. Paul, Minn., where he is connected with a large
mercantile establishment, and now resides at Minneapolis.

LULU COURTRIGHT ABBOTT, born Dec. 7, 1866, married Aug. 23, 1902,
Burton D. Herron, a prominent banker of Mt. Vernon, Ohio, now their
home.

She received her education in the schools of Mt. Vernon, and while
a girl lived on the farm of her father. They have issue:

Cornelia Courtright, b. Dec. 9, 1903.
John Abbott, b. Dec. 29, 1904.
Harriet, b. Oct. 8, 1906, d. Mar. 1, 1907.
Helen Johnson, b. Sept. 12, 1910.

GENERAL ASHER MINER, born Nov. 14, 1860; married Hetty McNair
Lonsdale, Nov. 6, 1889, is a native of Wilkes-Barre, Pa., where he was
educated. The Miner family trace their ancestry in England to Henry
Miner, who died in 1359, through Thomas the immigrant, who came to
America in 1630, and from Asher and Charles Miner, pioneer settlers of
the Wyoming Valley.

He enlisted in Company D, 9th Infantry, National Guard, in 1884,
promoted through the grades to Captain of the same Company; appointed
General Inspector of Rifle Practice, with rank of Colonel in 1895; commissioned Colonel of the 9th Regiment Infantry, in 1898; appointed Colonel
of the 9th Infantry, Mar. 7, 1916; on Aug. 16, appointed Colonel
of the 3rd Penna. Field Artillery serving on the Mexican Border, until
Mar., 1917; for duty in the World War, Colonel Miner answered the call

of the President, in command of the 3rd Penn. Field Artillery (later the 109th) and continued in command until wounded at Apremont, France, in the Argonne Forest, Oct. 4, 1918, his left leg being amputated below the knee. He participated in the Fismes Vesle defensive, and the Oise-Aisne and Meuse-Argonne offensives, and was one of six American officers in the war to receive both the distinguished Service medal, and the distinguished service cross, and of these was the only one wounded in action. He was honorably discharged from service Sept. 26, 1920, and on April 26th, 1921, was appointed Brigadier General, P. N. G., in command of the Fifty-Third Artillery Brigade.

He learned the milling business in early manhood and upon the death of his father became President of the Miner-Hillard Milling Company, operating at Miners Mills. He is President of the Wyoming National Bank, and identified with several other institutions of Wilkes-Barre, financial and social. He served one term in the Pennsylvania Legislature, session of 1906-7.

General Asher and Hetty McNair (Lonsdale) Miner, issue:

Helen Lea, b. Aug. 7, 1890, m. Dr. Edward Bixby, June 1, 1916.
Elizabeth Ross, b. May 31, 1892, m. Neil Chrisman, Apr. 26, 1916.
Robert Charles, b. Apr. 10, 1894.
Margaret Mercer, b. June 6, 1898.
Hetty Lonsdale, b. Feb. 27, 1903.

SIDNEY ROBY MINER, b. July 28, 1864; married Lydia Atherton Stites, June 25, 1909; and died June 14, 1913; received his education in Wilkes-Barre, and Harvard University, and later graduated from the University of Pennsylvania, as an attorney, an occupation he followed in Wilkes Barre, where he lived, until his early death.

He was greatly interested in the Wyoming Historical Society, in which he was an officer for several years, taking a very active part in its proceedings. He was courteous, refined, kind and considerate to all with whom he had dealings, and admired and respected for the many superior qualities of his heart and mind.

DR. CHARLES HOWARD MINER, born July 5, 1868; married June 1, 1904, Grace Lea Shoemaker, was educated in Wilkes-Barre, and Princeton University, and graduated in medicine, from the University of Pennsylvania, is a prominent physician now practicing in Wilkes-Barre where he makes his home. He is one of the physicians on the staff of the Wilkes-Barre Hospital, and is distinguished for his researches in tuberculosis, to which he has given much attention. He has issue:

Charles Howard, Jr., b. Dec. 27, 1908.
Stella Mercer Shoemaker, b. Mar. 31, 1912.

EMMA GRACE ABBOTT, married Nov. 21, 1895, Justin Latham, now lives in Sandwich, Ills., where her husband was a popular and successful merchant. Issue:
Wendell, b. Mar. 16, 1897.
Charlotte Miner, b. May 28, 1900.

ELIZABETH ABBOTT, married June 27, 1894, Dr. Frank E. David, makes her home in Chicago, where her husband is engaged in the practice of medicine. No children.

SARAH ABBOTT, married July 25, 1900, Dr. S. Marx White, now resides in Minneapolis, Minn., where her husband is identified with the Minnesota State University as an instructor. Issue:
Asher Miner, b. Aug. 1, 1901.
Elizabeth, b. May 8, 1903.
Mary, b. Dec. 23, 1906.

DR. EDWARD WELLS AND HELEN LEA (MINER) BIXBY, issue:
Edward Wells, b. Oct. 29, 1917.
Hetty Lonsdale, b. Feb. 3, 1920.

NEIL AND ELIZABETH ROSS (MINER) CHRISMAN, issue:
Hester Lonsdale, b. Mar. 3, 1917.
Neil, Jr., b. June 13, 1920.

James and his brother, Philip Abbott, who were nephews of John Abbott, killed by the Indians in '1778' were pioneer settlers at Scranton, the history of which says "James Abbott, then of Wilkes-Barre, but formerly of Windham, Conn., bought lot No. 30, and soon after lot No. 40, and with his brother Philip, were for several years among the most active and enterprising men in the township.

Philip Abbott built a grist mill on Roaring Brook in 1788, the first settlement of the kind in the vicinity. In October, his brother James joined him in the enterprise, and later, in the spring of 1789, Reuben Taylor was admitted to partnership. They also owned and operated the first saw mill there. Philip Abbott built his house in Scranton in 1788, in which year Reuben Taylor built the second house there."

The grist mill built and owned by Philip and James Abbott was the first industry established in Scranton.

REVOLUTIONARY SERVICES.

JOHN ABBOTT, a private in the 6th Company, 24th Regiment, Connecticut Militia, commanded by Capt. Resin Geer, who took part in battle of Wyoming, July 3, 1778, and was killed by the Indians, about the middle of August, 1778.

STEPHEN FULLER, (father-in-law of John Abbott) during the battle of Wyoming, was in the Fort to protect the women and children, the oldest man in the battle.

WILLIAM SEARLE, Sergeant, member of one of the Conn. Military Companies at Wyoming, injured while on a scouting party, prior to the battle of Wyoming. He was in charge of a party of women and children who were fleeing back to their homes in Conn., and the Minisink, soon after the battle.

CONSTANT SEARLE, captured and killed in the battle of Wyoming, July 3d, 1778, being one of the aged men who took part.

OBADIAH GORE, took part in the battle of Wyoming, being one of the old men in the Fort, for its defence.

DANIEL GORE, Lieut. and later Captain, took part in the battle of Wyoming, July 3, 1778, as Lieut. of the 6th Company, 24th Regiment, Connecticut Militia, and during the engagement, had an arm shot off. He also accompanied the Sullivan expedition to New York, in October, 1779.

BENJAMIN CORTRIGHT, served as a private, Class 3, of the 6th Battalion, Northampton (Penn.) County Militia, under the command of Col. Jacob Stroud and Capt. John Van Etten, as shown by the muster roll of May, 1778.

   He also was a private of the 1st Company, 5th Battalion, in 1780; the 4th Company, 5th Battalion, in 1781; and again in June, 1782, his name written variously as Cartright, Cortright, Curtright and Courtright.

JOHN KENNEDY, served as a private in the 4th Regiment, Orange County, (New York) Militia, and also in other Companies in Northampton County, Penn., guarding the frontiers from attacks by the Indians, at various times, during the Revolution.

CORTRIGHTS WHO SERVED IN THE REVOLUTION.

From New York:

   John Cortright, 4th Dutchess, Land Bounty Rights.
   Henry Cortright, 3d Tyron County, Land Bounty Rights.
   Henry Cortright, 2d Albany County Militia.
   John Cortright, 2d Albany County Militia.
   Henry Abraham Cortright, The Line, 2d Regiment.
   Henry Cortright, The Line, 4th Regiment.

Capt. Benjamin Cortright, 3d Regiment, Ulster County Militia.
Henry Cortright, 3d Regiment, Ulster County Militia.
Jacobus Cortright, 3d Regiment, Ulster County Militia.
Abraham Cortright, 3d Regiment, Ulster County Militia.
Mattheus Cortright, 3d Regiment, Ulster County Militia.
Capt. Moses Cortright, 3d Regiment, Orange County Militia.
Abraham Cortright, 4th Regiment, Orange County Militia.
Silvester Cortright, 2d Regiment, Ulster County Militia.
Lowrence Cortright, 3d Regiment Ulster County Militia.
Louwerens Cortright, Jr., 3d Regiment Ulster County Militia.
Harry Cortright, 3d Regiment, Tyron County Militia.
Hendrick A. Cortright, Bradt's Rangers.
Abraham V. Cortright, In Capt. Weisenfel's Company.

From New Jersey:

John Cortright, Major, 3d Battalion, Sussex County.
Henry W. Cortright, Captain, 3d Battalion, Sussex County.
Aaron Cortright, Captain, in Continental Army.
Thomas Cortright, Private, 3d Battalion, Sussex County Militia.
Jacob Cortright, Private, 3d Battalion, Sussex County Militia.
Jonas Cortright, Private, 3d Battalion, Sussex County Militia.
Solomon Cortright, Private, 3d Battalion, Sussex County Militia.

From Northampton County Pennsylvania:
May 14, 1778.
Muster Roll of 6th Battalion, 4th Company, under Capt. John Van Etten.

James, Henry, Benjamin, Abraham and Daniel Cortright.

Return of 5th Battalion, 1st Company, for 1780.

James, Gideon, Benjamin, Levi and Daniel Cortright.

Return of 5th Battalion, 3d Company, for June, 1781.

·   Henry, Benjamin, Abraham, Levi and Daniel Cortright.

Return of 5th Battalion for June, 1782,

Gideon, Benjamin, David, Levi, Cornelius and Daniel Cortright.

Also served in the 5th Battalion,

Jacobus, James, John, Walton and William Courtright.

Killed in the battle of Wyoming, July 3d, 1778,

John and Christopher Cortright.

The above names were spelled with variations by the mustering officers.

INDEX

De Forest, Henry, 16
  Isaac, 16
de Hooges, Anthony, 103, 104
De Key, Teunis, 29
Delamater, Hester, 18
  Isaac, 18
  Jan, 18
  John, 32, 34
  Margaret, 33, 34
  Margriet, 37
  Susanna, 32, 36
Delaval, John, 18
Delva, Antje, 51
de Meyer, Nicholas, 26
Dennemarken, Margaret, 97
  Margriet, 35, 39, 97
Dennington, Ruth, 84
Dennis, R. W., 99
Dennison, Nathan, Col., 115
  Sarah, 115
De Pue, Marritjen, 51
De Puy, Catharine, 46
  Catrina, 35, 40
des Marest, David, 18
Devoor, Aefie, 36, 37
  Effie, 37
  John, 33, 37
Dewis, Sherrill F., 81
de Wit, Mary, 31
De Witt, Jacob I., 38
  Jan, 51
  Mary, 35
Dickey, Cornelius R., 94
  Earl A., 94
  Frank A., 84, 94
Dieckle, M. Rachel, 76, 89
Diffenbacher, Sarah C., 65, 74
Dignon, Francis H., 95
  Frank J., 73, 86
  Sidney L., 95
  Sidney Le Grand, 86
Dildein, Annatje, 36, 41
Dingman Alida (or Huldah), 39, 46,
  97
Dingemans, Jacob, 103
Dircks, Madeleen, 50
  Magdaleen, 50
  Magdalena, 51
Ditwiler, Ethel M., 78, 90
Dodson, Mary, 97, 98
Dongan, Thomas, 27
  Thomas, Gov., 18
Dotterer, Davis H., 61, 69
  Louise, 69, 80
  William C., 69
Douglas, Ann, 112
  Elizabeth, 106
  John, 88
  William, 112
Drake, Effie, 39, 46, 97
  Elizabeth, 36

Draper, Hannah, 106, 107
  James, 106
  Moses, 106
  Nathan, 45, 56
Duane, Thomas, 108
Dubrock, Clara A., 74
Durkee, Capt. Robert, 109
Durgy, Martha, 113
  William, 113
Du Pay, Niclas, 50
Dutcher, Charles, 43
Dyckman, Cornelis, 30
  Jan, 14, 18, 19
  Wyntie, 30, 33
Dyer, Adele M., 88
Dymond, Hazel Alberta, 93
  John Henry, 93
  Lena Elmira, 93
  Stephen, 84, 93

Eaton, Robert, 73
Edgar, Martha, 41
Edgerton, Julia, 63, 71
  Mary, 63, 71
Edson, W. Q., 99
Edwards, Margaret, 98
Elderkin, John, 116
  Paltiah, 116
Elmer, Capt. Nathaniel, 101
Emmons, Catharina, 36
  Catharine, 41
  Lena, 45, 48
  Rebecca, 36, 41
Engburgh, Cora A., 70, 75, 118, 120
  Teckla, 70, 75, 118, 120
Ennes, Catharina, 44
  Cathrina, 38
  Cornelia, (Viervant), 54
  Jannetje, 35, 38, 54
  Jannetjen, 52
  William, 54
Emery, Margaret, 41
  William C., 114
Evans, Edward T., 72, 84
  Harriet Virginia, 84
  Marian L., 84
  Richard H., 84
Eleyessen, Bastiaen, 25, 26
  Metje, 25

Fairfield, Jennie A., 66, 75
Fanning, Edmund, 116
  Ellen (——), 116
  Marie, 116
Farmer, Margaret, 63, 71
Fearman, Frank D., 71
Fell, Edward, 109
  Jesse, 57
  Jesse, Judge, 109
  Judge, 42
Fenton, Abigail, 112

Wattell, John, 111
  Mary, 111
Waugh, Janet, 89
Webber, Hans, 27, 28, 49
Weeks, Harry V., 86, 96
  Helen B., 96
  John L., 96
  Louis, 74, 86
Welch, Constance, 114
Weld, Elizabeth, 106
  John, 106
  Joseph, Capt., 106
Wells, Alice Lee, 77
  Clara Ida, 68, 79
Wentz, Beryl C., 78
  James, 68, 78
  John Milton, 90
  Lee B., Lieut. 78,
  Milton H., 78, 00
Westbroek, Antje, 38
  Jacob, 103
  Maria, 103
Westbrook, A. J., 114
  Aaron, 43
  Antje, 44
  Evert Roos, 48
  Johannes, 97
  Joseph, 43, 46
Westerhout, Adrianus, 27
Westfael, Margriet, 38, 44
  Maria, 48
  Marya, 38
Westfal, Derick, 38
  Hendrick, 38
  Johanna, 103
Westfall, Abraham, 45
  Johannes, 34
  Plony, 48
Westpfahl, Matilda, 76, 88
Wetherbee, Hannah I., 114
Wheeler, Cecelia A., 86, 95
  Hannah, 115
  Isaac, 110, 116
  Margaret, 115
  Mary (——), 116
  Thomas, 116
  William, 116
White, Asher Miner, 122
  C. Frank, 80
  Charles A., 69
  Elizabeth, 122
  Grace R., 80
  Henry C., 69, 80
  John, 61, 69
  Joshua L., 69
  Laura M., 80
  Margaret B., 69, 80
  Mary, 122
  S. Marx, Dr., 120, 122
  Sarah E., 69, 80
Wilcox, Samuel, 106

Wilds, Francis, 41
William, Duke of Juliers, 10
  of Orange, 11
Williams, Asher, 81
  Bernice S., 92
  Blanche, 81
  Clarissa, 58, 60
  Elizabeth C., 92
  Evan R., 81, 92
  Gilbert, 81
  Gladys I., 92
  Harry E., 92, 96
  Henry, 81
  Henry F., 61, 70
  Isaac, 113
  Jean M., 92
  John, 44, 103
  John W., 70, 81
  Lydia, 81
  Margaret L., 92
  Marion Elizabeth, 96
  Milton, 92
  Paul S., 92
  Robert, 81
  Roger, 111
  Rose, 96
  Rose C., 70, 81, 92
  Samuel, 38
  Sheldon R., 92
Wilson, John D., 82
Windfield, James, 43
Windsor, Geneva E., 78
  George B., 68, 78
  George Wayne, 78
  Helen G., 78, 90
  Hester M., 78, 90
  Jessie Ruth, 78
  Laura Pearl, 78
  Leetha L., 78
  Lillith B., 78
  William Deane, 78
Wing, Allison G., 88
  Grace V., 71, 75, 83, 87
  Wendell C., 88
Wintermout, Jurian, 38
Witter, Hannah, 107, 110, 111
  Josiah, 107, 110
  William, 107, 110
Wolfe, Freeborn, 113
  Peter, 113
Wolters, Kier, 30
Wood, Rena, 82, 93
Woodruff, Matilda, 114
Worley, Margaret Z., 76
Wright, Albert O., 71
  Bonnie, 82
  Charles F., 63, 71
  Charles M., 59
  Charles Miner, 63
  Chester, 71
  Edward, 71

Made in the USA
Middletown, DE
06 November 2018